THe
Color
of the
Sunset

MARIE MASTERS

authorHOUSE®

AuthorHouse™
1663 Liberty Drive
Bloomington, IN 47403
www.authorhouse.com
Phone: 1-800-839-8640

Cover Designed by Denise Weisgerber.

Monet art provided by Aweseome Art, Windsor, California.

Cliff Walk at Pourville art provided by Encore Editions, New Hope, Pennsylvania.

Published by AuthorHouse   01/31/2012

ISBN: 978-1-4685-4967-6 (sc)
ISBN: 978-1-4685-4966-9 (hc)
ISBN: 978-1-4685-4965-2 (ebk)

Library of Congress Control Number: 2012902072

Acknowledgements

Thanks to John and Lynn Kinch for their encouragement
on early drafts.

Special thanks to Patricia Miller, whose insight artfully
refined the manuscript.

Finally, thanks to Daniel Minock, author of *Thistle Journal:
And Other Essays* and editor of this text.

Prologue

Ibelieve in the power of coincidence. Take my first byline in a major newspaper: it was situated directly under a picture of Claude Monet's water lilies.

Placed in the front of the real estate section, below the fold and below the Monet artwork, "A Home Is What You Make of It" discussed transforming a beige-upon-beige apartment into "my little piece of the sky," a metaphor for rebuilding and colorizing my life after divorce. Above the essay, blurred splotches of pink, white and green floated there in a tiny computer-captured image of one of Monet's most recognized works.

Since I clipped only the art and the essay, not the whole page, I can't recall whether the article accompanying the water lilies talked about trends in gardens, shower curtains or dinner plates. Nothing was too commercial when it came to using the now-familiar design, which appeared everywhere during the 1990s in a peculiar centennial homage to Monet's fame a hundred years before.

The framed clipping still hangs near my writing desk to remind me that anything is possible and that mystical forces are at work. A week before my essay's publication, I did a creative writing exercise that asked, "If you could interview anyone alive or dead, who would it be?" I first jotted down Abraham Lincoln. Cliché, I know. Then I wrote Charlie Chaplin and Claude Monet, as I told the truth about who I'd really like to corner in a coffee shop for an hour or two.

Later, when I picked up a paper at the drugstore and saw my essay in the Detroit Free Press beneath Monet's water flowers, I shivered with recognition of my connection with this great artist by the juxtaposition of my writing and Monet's artwork. For nearly twenty years, I had been drawn to Monet's signature light-infused style at museums, but now there was this pairing in the newspaper. I had asked the universe for some time near him, and this was pretty close. I still did not know that Claude Monet would become more than just a favorite artist of mine. Over the next decade, through the bumpy journey of living alone again (actually, living alone for the first time), he would posthumously become my mentor.

I would also acknowledge his influence during most of my tempestuous sixteen-year marriage. Framed prints did more than splash color on otherwise barren walls in our marital home. Monet's landscapes gave me focus or distraction, whatever I needed most.

Monet's work has always been more than purely decorative for me. Maybe one of my living, breathing mentors said it best after reading a first draft of this manuscript. He said, "This book should be subtitled, 'How Art Saved My Life.'"

"Wherever I go, graffiti reminds me of home and the notion that art cannot be contained. It can only be expressed."

Chapter 1

Mardi Gras (c. 1960s & 1970s)

My world before Claude Monet was steel blue. Gunmetal gray. Camouflage green. The color of machinery. My hometown's name, Roseville, was a misnomer, with its harsh square grids of streets and rows of ranch homes. There was no abundance of roses, except in my mother's well-tended garden. I don't remember any significant parks in this bedroom community, except industrial parks with tool shops housing smoke-sputtering machines that sheered metal and extruded plastic into car parts. In nearby Detroit, gray and brown skyscrapers, weather-wasted houses and spray-can art.

Graffiti has its own raw beauty. I've seen it all my life when driving through the city of Detroit. And whenever I take the train to Chicago, the tracks run through a virtual outdoor gallery of colorful words and cartoon-like pictures as we approach Union Station. Wherever I go, graffiti reminds me of home and the notion that art cannot be contained. It can only be expressed.

Early on, I exhibited a talent for excessive art silliness, sketching rabbits with too-large ears and dogs with tongues spastically protruding from their snouts. In grade school, kids sat near me to see what ridiculousness my "art" would render next. Teachers did not appreciate this talent. That familiar clenched jaw look meant I should return to reading about the anti-climactic adventures of Dick and Jane (yawn and stare out the window as the two dreary protagonists played ball with Spot and visited a "real" farm).

Then in ninth grade, my first French class artistically liberated me. I don't recall being introduced to Claude Monet while taking this class with a jet-haired Greek woman named Miss Stamatelos, unless his work graced her disheveled bulletin board. But Miss Stamatelos demanded that I speak French every day and hang onto her every utterance, lest she would lob a chalkboard eraser in my direction. Even under such duress, I managed to create my first work of notable art in her class.

My first English-to-French publication boasted a unique use of construction paper tied together with chunky yellow yarn. Various hues of paper differentiated sections of the rough-hewn booklet. Red and orange pages depicted fashion items clipped from magazines, and captions written in English and French described the pictures. Brown and green paper featured things in nature, such as African elephants and roses, such opposites oddly paired together for no particular reason.

My attempt at a French picture book might not have impressed the likes of Claude Monet, but it did garner third-prize in the Arts and Sciences Fair at Edgar A. Guest Junior High. I never claimed my prize. When the eraser whizzed by my head as Miss Stamatelos announced we had a winner in our midst, I thought the chalk obliterator was intended for someone else's noggin, so someone else must have won. Momentarily, I relished the idea that she missed and felt a small victory.

Then, while looking squarely into my eyes, she angrily growled through her teeth, "Someone in our class won third prize. And had she been at the fair, would have received a ribbon."

There was a ribbon? I didn't know she entered my floppy paged book of many colors. She had suggested my parents take me to the fair, but I was never sure why. I probably found my way to a street baseball game after school on fair day; playing in the street let us dodge cars and thumb our noses at drivers. Mom might have been chasing my cute but active six-year-old sister. And Dad worked 16-hour days at his tool-and-die business. He often ate a plate of eggs for dinner while watching the 11 o'clock news. I doubted he had time.

That same school year, I also took perspective drawing. The art teacher was a tall, fragile-looking man with a four o'clock shadow at eight o'clock in the morning. He expressed intense concern for every pottery ashtray that exploded in his kiln. "You've got to get the air out," he dramatically tsk-tsk'd every time he opened the kiln to find another ashtray fired to smithereens. It was like he had found a dead body. I'm positive this fear of killing ashtrays is what has kept me from pursuing fine arts all these years.

I kept drawing, though. I mean, how much damage could I do with a pencil? Despondent from the pottery we demolished, the same lanky and muttering art teacher who tried to teach us the joys of ashtray sculpture shuffled around the room, looking for pieces of fruit, bottles, boxes, anything that had shape or form. With these everyday items, he constructed the ugliest possible still-lifes. Nothing I drew could improve his blasé compositions. Still, an apple never looked bigger than a bucket or a wine bottle, and for that, I thank him.

It was a middle-school drafting teacher, however, who finally nixed my artistic ambitions. The engineer-turned-instructor hovered like a hornet. We waited for his stinging comments, disappointed hum and accompanying head-shake to show his dislike. I'm convinced that's why people don't sit down and draft. You stand up at attention, waiting for the buzz that surely comes to tell you what you did wrong.

"You're not designing a skyscraper, for God's sake. Just keep the lines smooth and straight," he reminded. "Twirl your pencil. That's it, twirl your pencil so it stays sharp as you run it along the ruler."

I can still draw a straight line, while sharpening a pencil at a ruler blade, with the best of them.

Claude Monet and Impressionism were not yet familiar to me when I reached high school. But like Dorothy searching for her Emerald City, I sought a colorized and fantastical world beyond the rainbows that arched even over the lunch-bucket city of Roseville from time to time. I began craving "the good things."

*　　*　　*

By the time I could drive, I couldn't wait to get away from my hometown. Residential homes were tucked in between industrial "parks," a strange reference considering the environmental pollution these businesses created when shaping metal and plastic into parts that fed hungry assembly lines. During the Sixties and Seventies, mom-and-pop businesses (my mother's and father's included) cropped up near such suburbs, so people could escape man-eating factories and work minutes from home in smaller spin-offs of the Big Three automotive factories.

In our neighborhood, homes were built in a few basic designs, the only distinction between them the color of the brick—red, gray, yellow-ish, or pink. There was a nurturing claustrophobia to this cookie-cutter sameness. Once I'd seen a few of my friends' homes, I had seen them all. Most suburbanites were living the dream just by owning one, but it wasn't my dream. I lacked the "go industrial" gene and developed a healthy disrespect for the people who worked with metal and machines just to pay a mortgage. My mother claimed, "You always thought you were better than the rest of us." The truth was that terms like Luxury Sedans, Captains of Industry, and Gross National Product meant nothing to me. I was a kid, and these concepts were too huge for my pea brain.

To escape, I took teenage loner trips in my first car, a dented and dinged Pontiac Bonneville that was more like a boat on wheels. I'd drive to Lexington, a town situated on a stretch of beach located an hour north of Detroit and its suburbs. There I sat on the dock, sketched pictures of driftwood and wrote terrible poetry. "Earthy claws pulling at me" may have reflected my perceptions, but no one wanted to read about mental and emotional stagnation. My English teacher was torn between entering this melodramatic poem in a newspaper-sponsored contest and sending me to the one-and-only school counselor (after all, it was the Seventies, and not everybody had his or her designated psychologist yet). "Is everything okay with you?" this chronically hyperactive teacher worried, as if I had contemplated suicide.

I only tried to express how sometimes other people's expectations run counter to those we have for ourselves, I assured her. If I had to explain the "claws" reference today, I'd say it's like a Pterodactyl snatching up a player in a virtual reality game; other people's ideas swoop down from nowhere and dictate, "This is what you must learn in school" and "You will work as a bookkeeper or a corporate secretary." I'd rather have been carried off by a giant Pterodactyl to The Lost World than to work in a dead-end automotive-related job.

My parents complained that my head was always "in the clouds." Writing and drawing pictures, they explained, would not make me a living.

There were lots of people—an entire middle class—making plenty of money at the auto companies back then. It was true. But no one saw the people behind the scenes of slick designs trotted out with a buxom blond on the hood at auto shows. A good friend of mine delivered blueprints between Chrysler plants on the midnight shift. For this, she received $25 an hour, discounts on a vehicle necessary to do her job, and she dropped out of school. My boyfriend drove a truck delivering many-ton machine parts that would be installed on automotive assembly lines. I took a job encoding the magnetic strips of credit cards at Manufacturer's Bank. I qualified because of my rapid typing skill.

Living the blue-collar life meant partying with likewise career-stunted friends. Lost weekends featured beer, wine, marijuana, large quantities of Doritos and rock music amped up to room-shaking levels to erase memories of the work week . . . machines stamping parts, saws buzzing through metal, phones ringing endless orders for parts, and other annoyingly repetitive sounds programming our brains. Anesthetized by drugs and alcohol, card games helped us stay giddy and coherent enough to drive home.

As an alternative to these same-old-thing weekends, another escape from the ho-hum might include "cruising" Jefferson Avenue, a road that sidled the Detroit River and led out of the city and into affluent suburbs called "The Pointes." The e-ending evoked what was ostentatious and European. After all, the city of Detroit (DAY-TOI) had French beginnings. Automotive money families lived in Grosse Pointe, Grosse Pointe Farms, Grosse Pointe Park and Grosse Pointe Shores—Ford and other big auto money names.

Art must have covered the walls of their mansions, some with servants' cottages bigger than my family's ranch home, but I never saw any of it. Each monolithic home sat back from the lakeshore drive, and front yards warded off trespassers with privet hedges and brick-and-mortar walls. For all the blandness outside, I imagined glorious profusions of color and artful embellishments inside.

Jefferson Avenue found fame in Clint Eastwood's 2008 movie *Gran Torino*. In the film, A Hmong boy, who is bequeathed the dead hero's prized vehicle, tools down the lakeshore as if he has finally realized success by possessing the classic car. Seeing the movie brought back memories of countless rides with my nose pressed against a friend's used-car window to see what rich people had that I did not: gardeners, elbow-rubbing cocktail parties and "No Through Traffic" signs. We could look, but only from a distance. I wanted to touch and possess this lifestyle.

*   *   *

The first time I cruised, my foxy friend Patty wore enough cheap perfume to drown anyone within several yards. She smelled clean and fresh, like tropical fruit. We were hormonal and looking for boys to notice us. But if I was vanilla—and I might have been with a cherry on top my only flavor enhancer—Patty was pineapple-mango surprise. Boys could not help but notice her, which was one of the reasons I put up with her self-indulgence and the fact that she borrowed my clothes and looked better in them than I did. She wiggled that beautifully sleek and tanned body. Her skin shone like luminescent silk. And her thick auburn hair swung this-way-and-that when she walked. She was my ticket out of the boredom. That night, one look at Patty's mischievous smile told me to hang on tight for the carnival ride that would follow.

She had found an older boy to drive us down Jefferson. She sat in the front seat of the beat-up but clean Dodge Dart with the driver, who treated us girls like we were equals, even if I was sequestered into the back seat when Patty winked in John's direction and then pushed the seat down and ushered me next to a nameless boy who raised his hand to wave me in rather than to look at me. I didn't have Patty's sheen, scent, and cosmetics acumen. The back-seat passenger made that clear by ignoring me.

If my so-called date that night had a name, it didn't matter. When we hit Jefferson, a Midwestern Camelot rushed by the car window, and nothing and nobody else mattered. The moon shone on the water, glistening tiny waves and ripples and whitening the foam at the shoreline. It didn't seem fair that Pointes people had more stars than those hovering over my postage-stamp backyard. Homes didn't have a single porch light like the one Dad left on until I got home; their closely clipped bushes, topiary trees, and outdoor *objets d'art* had special lighting to showcase the grounds. I squinted at well-lit cavernous rooms inside, trying to see people eating canapés or sipping champagne.

Patty jolted me back from a dreamer's fog. There was that glint again. "Take off your shirt. C'mon, take it off right now. Do it with me, please," she begged, while jerking up her shirt until her belly showed. She stopped below the bra line. "C'mon. Ready?"

I looked at her near-perfect body and imagined perky breasts ready to spring out. I had more of everything under my shirt and was not sure it would be fully appreciated.

The no-name boy next to me smiled for the first time, as if to say, *Go ahead. Maybe the evening won't be a complete loss.* Then he dared me. "Do it. What, you afraid?"

Meantime, the driver glanced over his shoulder. He wore a half-smile because he knew Patty would do it, but would I? He seemed to be waiting more for me to disrobe as if he knew it was my first time exposing my everything. He didn't want to miss my corruption.

"Okay," I said, prodding Patty along. Poising my hands at my shirt's hem as if ready to yank it off, I said, "Let's go."

"All right. Ready, set . . . one, two, three," said Patty, whose spirited laugh filled the car. Her stark white bra turned neon in the darkness. Half-naked, she bopped to the Beach Boys on the radio and risked getting a ticket for indecent exposure. She waved her shirt out the window and howled like that stiff-collared neighborhood probably never heard before. "Good, good, good, good vibrations," she defiantly sang as loudly as she could.

My lips were not moving, but I sang every word with her.

"You didn't take yours off," Patty said when the song stopped and she quit bouncing around the front seat. But she didn't really care. The attention had been hers, and she made us all feel free for a minute.

Ironically, the boy in the front seat with Patty became my first husband when I was one month shy of eighteen. The marriage would last a whopping three years—one of those "girl has first kiss and thinks it's love" things. We thought we knew love; we only knew the basest sensations and vibrations. Apparently, his over-the-shoulder look had noted how I would not undress before strangers, only him. But John did . . . undress in front of strangers, that is. Too many of them. I played demure wife to his cavalier, rock-star persona until I could not anymore. Did I mention he was desperately good-looking in a hippie sort of way?

I recently learned the meaning of regret. It is not the mistakes I made, such as marrying a high-school fling who made my hormonal motor whir. I don't regret the first and only time I drank whiskey, which resulted in spending the night using the toilet rim as a life preserver. John sweetly covered my shoulders with a bath towel, said good-night and left me there.

I regret not taking off my shirt that first night I cruised Jefferson with Patty, John and Whoever He Was. Not doing so has led to a more conventional life. I cared too much about the disappointment in my mother's eyes when I came in late and about dispelling the rumors sure to fly at school the following Monday. I wish John would have taken me home that night instead of Patty, never to take her out again because he knew he couldn't tame her. She was a fox or a tiger, wild and feline. Instead, I was a cocker spaniel, eager to please and obey. Easy prey.

Given another chance, I'd do things differently. If I could go back, I'd let my spirit soar and proudly flash my freak flags in a single life-affirming Mardi gras moment.

Claude Monet. *La Corniche Near Monaco*. 1884. (Oil on canvas, 75 x 94 cm.) Rijksmuseum, Amsterdam.

Chapter 2

Sea-Escapes (c. 1980)

*I*t is nine years later. I'm only twenty-four years old, and I've been married . . . divorced . . . . and I'm already remarried to someone else for the past two years. I'm looking at a painting that I like, but I don't know the artist. I never pictured myself in Europe. Everything here is foreign to me. Maybe that's what draws me back to the simple complexity of the painting. Up close, the brush strokes are wide—knife strokes really—each looking like a separate tile in a mosaic. Only from a distance can I distinguish a sea-scape.

I am in a Netherlands museum and have never seen anything like this frantic attempt at capturing shimmers of a single moment. The water reminds me of Holland's soggy but gorgeous environs, but the work is not painted in the photographic manner of some other artists. Reality is not the artist's forte. Nor is it mine. Escapism, that's the thing. The artist's style is sketchy, not precise. Rocks are only implied, terra firma dabbed in terra cotta. The grass, which looks like random scratches when I'm close, depicts the breeze having its way with the greenery, waving it back and forth, as I step back. I hear water crashing from the splotchy turquoise sea. The scene has a soulful, infinite quality, each stroke a mere pixel in a grander universe.

I lose sense of time as I'm pulled into the visual vortex of the artist's dappled blues, greens and oranges, all swirled together into one breath-halting composition. I want to roll around in nature's colors. I have never seen *waves depicted as feathery wisps, nor slight brush-sweeps of white clouds passing by . . . seemingly moving, not stagnant or standing still.*

Though I still don't know its name, this painting is a splash of lightness amidst the darkness of other European portraits. Not a window or ray of sunlight in those. There must be at least a flickering candle near the subjects' somber faces, invariably posing right or left. I'm tired of their judgmental looks. The painting on which I focus is effervescent, expansive from one end of the canvas to the other. It explodes with life. I smell the sandy air and feel the tiny shells crackle beneath my bare feet. The scene smacks of summertime at Lake Huron back in Michigan, as I aimlessly wander amidst toe-kissing waves. I am homesick.

*   *   *

My husband Joe was instantly jealous when I fell in love with my first Monet. He wanted to rush me through the Netherlands museum that was one of our first stops during a European honeymoon taken two years after our wedding. That's why I don't remember the painting's name. I needed time to linger, soak in the scene Monet had created for me. Joe broke the spell by whispering, "That's stupid."

Ah, yes, I had let my stupidity show by not paying attention to a painting of his choice. During our "twenty-one countries in twenty-one days" excursion, my job was to follow him from castles to cathedrals to statues mapped out in what I called the "godforsaken Fodor's guide." He led the way in museums, too, since I didn't know Renoir from Michelangelo. "What'd did you say his name is again, MO-NAY"?

"We came here to see Rembrandt," Joe said. "You don't come to Holland to see Monet. You come to see the Dutch Masters."

It was moments like these that made me wonder what we were doing together. Marriage on the rebound felt more like bouncing up-and-down on a yo-yo collared around my neck than playing basketball with a nice duck-and-weave momentum. I was drawn back into the madness of not living my own life. True, I did not recognize Dutch painters, but I knew what I liked.

"Are you coming or not?" Joe looked around as if I was the one who had shouted and ruined the Zen of other art patrons now staring at us.

In hindsight, maybe I should have said, "Not," and headed back to the States while I had the chance, instead of following Joe into the darker galleries and recesses of the museum. Like the Mona Lisa wearing a rubber nose, now that my lack of culture was showing, he had even more ammunition to make me feel inadequate.

*   *   *

My first European vacation was a gift from Joe's parents. Strange, since they never forgave us for eloping.

His parents were both English, the first generation born in Canada, and they were big on ceremony, especially weddings. His Mum's lilting speech made even admonishments pleasant. I barely felt the barb when she suggested that the only reason Joe would have married me must have been an illegitimate baby. "Joe knows his responsibilities. He will do the right thing." She paused, allowing me to reveal a due date that did not exist.

Joe and I married because our previous relationships didn't work. We needed something that did. Maybe we needed too much. I already had the white-dress Catholic ceremony with Marriage #1, so Joe and I would foot the wedding bill this time. It was the photographer who tipped the scale toward elopement, asking for $500 that neither Joe nor I could produce on our student's and secretary's income. We decided against the photographs, the band, the festively decorated restaurant and the off-white satin dress that draped like fabric champagne behind me. Eloping was cheaper. A pink sweater and beige skirt would do.

We woke up the next morning in a curtains-drawn Niagara Falls hotel room, with a large bottle of Baby Duck sparkling wine emptied and laying on the nightstand. My hair was a tousled mess, and Joe woke up half-smiling through an alcohol-induced stupor.

My parents had witnessed the marriage in the judge's chambers, but Joe's parents only knew we disappeared for three days. "It will be fine," he said.

Which part? The part where we didn't tell them I was already married before or the part where we neglected to get their blessing on our new nuptials?

To my surprise, his parents celebrated our impromptu wedding with a small reception hosted in their well-appointed but a-bit-too-cozy living room. This unhappy little scene offered the perfect opportunity for family chastisement for my sins of omission. How would Mum do it? Properly, of course. She would drop the S-bomb to destroy our too-brief bliss. Just the way his mother said "Stephanie" implied his former girlfriend was as indulgent as Joe had told me. Stephanie would not have settled for less than a ballroom, twenty-piece band, and a designer gown for her wedding. That became obvious. As for a weekend honeymoon, are you kidding?

"I saw Stephanie at the mall the other day," Mum said only minutes after congratulating us.

There was sudden silence and everyone froze like frames in an old movie reel. Talking might have started a landslide of negativity and criticism . . . what they really thought of me, questions they really wanted to ask. So, I said nothing.

Joe studied his shoes at the mention of her name, choosing not to look at me or his mother.

Princess Stephanie would be "surprised by your news," Mum said. She was still going to university, don't you know . . . and on and on, until Stephanie's presence suffocated me in the small room full of strangers already stifling my ability to eek out a single complete sentence.

I had known about girls like Stephanie my whole life. Their coats matched their hats, which matched their dresses and dyed-to-match shoes. They had canopy beds and pictures of themselves scattered on their dainty dressers. I pictured her tucking long, honey locks over a porcelain shoulder, her smile model straight after a decade of braces, and finger and toe-nails painted a trendy shade of pink (which non-coincidentally complemented her polo shirt). She probably played tennis or kicked her shapely legs ever-so-high as head cheerleader at some high-brow school. She might as well have stamped "self-esteem" on her forehead or her ass, any place the world could readily see how wonderful she was.

Now that their Joe-and-Stephanie dreams had dissipated like smoke, his parents would do the next best thing—make us a worldly, well-traveled couple, or else show me how I didn't measure up in Stephanie's shadow.

When my new in-laws announced their gift of a European vacation eighteen months later, they refused to lump Great Britain with the rest of "The Continent." Further evidence of their British pride could be found in coffee-table books depicting the royal family. Joe's parents discussed the courtship of Charles and Diana with the familiarity of close relatives. On any given Sunday afternoon, a pot of Earl Grey tea steeped on the counter, a plate of cookies nearby—the kind that required dunking to prevent a broken tooth. Ginger snaps were my favorite. One final, careful swig of tea and cookie residue proved I knew better than to slurp.

During what started as a normal Sunday visit, where she typically didn't speak to me except to say hello and good-bye, his mother said, "We have something important to discuss with you."

I braced myself, ready for her to tell me the marriage was over.

We were all waiting for the tea to ripen, except Joe's father, who had other plans. Poppy (nicknamed by his grandkids) pointed a finger in the air, directing us not to move until he returned. When he did, he held out a tray with four stemmed glasses and a bottle of wine.

Poppy and I winked at each other, both of us imagining the nullifying effects the wine would have on the announcement that would follow. But Mum would not waste the Earl Grey. "No, I think tea is a better choice, Dear. It's the middle of the day," she said, genuinely disgusted.

Poppy's lower lip stuck out. His six-foot-three body folded into a pouting slump, and he left the room to stow the wine. His face contorted with stern resignation as he returned again with steaming tea in a flowered pot and china cups.

"That's better," said Mum, who poured as if serving the Queen herself. That was her motto about throwing parties, too: "Always prepare as if the Queen of England is coming." Cloth napkins. Sugar cubes. Tiny spoons.

I wasn't a royal. Joe wasn't a prince. And poor Poppy . . . his King of the Castle's position diminished with each bitter sip of tea he endured.

Once spoons quit clanking and first sips were taken, Mum presided. "Well, we're very proud that Joe will be graduating soon."

Poppy yawned and scratched his bald spot to see if it was still there.

"And you never had a proper honeymoon."

Did she say this to be nice, or was this a criticism of the way we entered into our marriage? I never could tell a dig from a compliment.

"So, Poppy and I have decided to send you on a trip. To Europe."

"Europe?" I said as if the thought never crossed my mind, because it had not.

Joe's sardonic smile revealed his thoughts of entitlement. *Thanks for finally noticing and rewarding me. Took you long enough.*

"We're going to Europe?" I repeated. One would think this would have been excellent news, but we were planning a move in a couple months. Joe took an engineering job in Illinois, and we were getting away from my hometown near Detroit, his hometown in Windsor and, hopefully, from Mum's inconvenient phone calls every time we fell into bed together.

Mum was excited enough for all of us. She took a half-bite of a cookie and placed the crumbling remains haphazardly on a table-top, forgetting her own rules that the coffee table was forbidden for feet, food and grandchildren's sticky fingers. As if by magic, she reached behind her and produced a bright-red brochure touting the benefits of seeing Europe by train, each city's station highlighted by a star. "You can go anywhere you want in Europe. There are dining and sleeping cars," she said, wiping the crumbs off the brochure and handing it to us.

"You'll see all the great cathedrals of Europe," chimed Poppy, who worked as an architect who specialized in churches. "I'll be happy to stow away."

"When are we leaving?" I said, worried about being whisked off again. I was still recovering from our hurry-up trip to Niagara Falls, followed by a year of cross-continental travel that was part of Joe's internship with Chrysler Canada.

"That's the best part. Go whenever you want." She licked her crumb-laden finger clean and then pointed at the number on the flier. "Call when you're ready. Three weeks starts when you get there. Get on and off the train whenever you like. Stay wherever you like. It's the trip of a lifetime."

"You've got to see Cologne Cathedral." Poppy showed signs of life again, perked up by the tea's caffeine. He searched a pile of books for the right one and began turning pages and pointing out what he would see if he were going.

However, Mum was done with us and cut short Poppy's travel-tips presentation. "Well, that was it . . . what we wanted to talk to you about. So, now you can start getting ready." She stood up and ushered us out. "You must have lots to do, what with the move and now the trip." We were the proud recipients of a three-week train pass to Europe, and now we should let her get on with her life. "Don't forget to sample the pastries when you're there," she said, munching the rest of her ginger snap. "They're to die for. You're going to love it."

Joe hugged her, and he started to hug his father, who likewise had popped a cookie into his mouth to quiet himself after being so rudely interrupted. But Poppy only reached out his hand. His father put his larger paw on his son's and held it there a minute. "You're welcome, son. We'll talk more before you leave." I knew they never would.

"Thank you so much," I unenthusiastically said.

Mum pulled me in for a hug with such force, it felt like we might actually be connecting. Then she jettisoned me away from her like a measuring tape sent back inside its steel shell. I'm still not sure if we had a close moment or not.

*   *   *

Soon, our dream trip became too realistic. Additional costs rapidly surpassed the original train fare. There were hotels and inns to book. For towns where we didn't call ahead, we would sleep in a spare bedroom of someone's home or find a youth hostel, sometimes separated in male and female quarters. One night we took the room above a bar and listened to all-night revelers. We discovered too late, the next morning, that the town had celebrated the anniversary of its liberation by Canadian forces in one of the world wars. Had we known, they could have brought the noisy conga line through our room. Might as well. Joe was Canadian, and I was living in Canada and couldn't sleep anyway.

We took the cheapest possible flight to Amsterdam. Only chickens and goats would have made it more authentically Third World. Once in Europe, three meals a day turned into two. We were so hungry in Luxembourg, when the server brought a filled-to-the-brim soup tureen with enough to feed everyone in the room, we ate it all. It was her fault. Couldn't she see the starvation in our greedy North American eyes? She disappeared into the kitchen, and when she returned for the tureen, we had finished a second bowl and had begun a third. I still hate lima bean soup.

Culture shock met us every time we departed the train, which happened often in twenty-one days. We would jump off, snap a picture and leap back on. In Ghent, Belgium, I suffered nausea in a medieval castle's musty basement torture chamber. In Utrecht, Holland, I found another type of torture by using a wooden bench toilet, with nothing more than a hole leading to defecation hell. One morning I followed a man who stunk up the bathroom with his scent and his stogie. Cigar ashes piled high on the floor. A cootie-covered newspaper was left behind.

There were extraordinary moments, too. We never made it as far as France, only Italy. In Venice, postcard streets boasted buildings pouring into the canals in various shades of ecru, brick, and gold. The morning air sung with a tenor voice belting out an aria. Later, a businessman on the waterbus serenaded us all the way back to the hotel. Affordable cappuccino became lunch. Not a coffee drinker before the trip, my addiction to the rich and creamy concoction began here. We discussed at length the quality of the foam. Getting piled-high milk was like finding the prize in Cracker Jacks. It made me feel excited, lucky.

The first night in Venice, I witnessed my first bidet. "Why is this toilet so low to the floor," I asked. "And there's no seat."

My exhausted husband, who had thrown himself across the bed, dragged himself up to investigate. Wiping open his eyelids, he corrected me. "That's not a toilet. It's a bidet."

"A what?"

"A bidet . . . for washing up."

"Washing up what?"

His part-naughty smile said it all.

I turned the handle and water shot up into the air. "Oh, you're kidding, right?"

Now even European bathroom fixtures conspired to show my ignorance. I fell belly-first onto the bed. So did he. We laughed ourselves to sleep.

Thirty years later, Switzerland still remains the most beautiful country I've ever seen in springtime. Every tree flowered. If Monet had been there, his paintbrush would have lustily gathered up the whispery pinks and vivid whites of millions of opening buds. In the distance, a spire of a small castle added a fairytale quality to the scenic panorama of snow-capped mountains, blue skies and a sea of blossoms. A boating excursion on Lake Lucerne will forever represent heaven for me. The colorful sails of boats floated in and out of a haze turned veil-like by the morning's bright sunshine. Just like the Monet painting that caught my eye at the start of our journey, now I was part of such an idyllic watery scene.

*   *   *

Back home, I pulled on my washed-out blue jeans and settled into a life of faking it. The honeyed moon too quickly set, and with each new sunrise, we moved ever-larger fractions away from each other.

Joe was once excited by life's possibilities. Married, he became dark and brooding as a neon purple sky outlining a solemn, intimidating mountain range. Gorgeous with that wavy black hair and steely blue eyes, his moods were distant, intense, and cool as a night breeze that prickles the skin and nothing more. Maybe I did this to him; made him serious about the work of life, and not joyous about its grandeur.

Joe's parents were right. The trip changed us. Joe became aware of a world of desires beyond our doorstep. As for me, I was haunted by the memory of my new favorite artist, Claude Monet, capable of creating such beauty. Now I knew a man could express love. Just not for me. Not now.

Chapter 3

Flashback (c. 2009 back to 1977)

*W*alking past the doors and throwing a glance over her shoulder, Camille Monet wears a tomato-hued scarf over her head, around her shoulders, and atop a charcoal dress. To paint The Red Kerchief, *Claude Monet plants his easel in the gray room and looks out through French doors to the garden, now bland from the cold. The beige-gold plants are dormant, gone to seed. The sheer white curtains framing her as she sashays by the window add to the gray-speckled wallpaper and wheat-textured floor with another layer of colorlessness.*

I wonder what it's like to be the splash of red in the painter's otherwise muted palette. The picture's duotone composition captures the fire of their brief relationship, cut short by her untimely death a short time later. But what makes Monet happy now? I fantasize it is Camille as she passes by the window, bringing fiery joy to an otherwise gloomy day. The object of the artist's affection seems clear. Camille offers life-giving color to his bleak world. Other women may attract his eye, but she captures his imagination with her unmistakable brightness. She is the one, not just anyone to paint.

The large-as-life canvas depicts Madame Monet as mysterious. Are the eyes brown or blue? Are the cheeks rosy-round or merely flushed? Quick dabs of paint reveal her coquettish mood. Perhaps Claude and Camille made love earlier, and she bundles up to walk and refresh herself. Maybe he wants her right then.

*   *   *

In January 2009, the Detroit Institute of Arts temporarily hosted The Cleveland Museum of Art's "Monet to Dali" exhibition while the Ohio museum renovated its facility. To my surprise, the exhibit featured a nearly life-size painting of *The Red Kerchief.* I was mesmerized by the love unfolding between Claude and Camille. It had been fourteen years since I divorced Joe, and I had no such crimson moment committed to memory.

I first saw Monet's *The Red Kerchief* on a calendar my sister Susan gave me one Christmas. With its lack of garden-delight colors, the work stood out from other Monet landscapes. No blue spotless skies poured down on the green, grassy fields and leafy poplars. No rich browns and coral dripped off rocky cliffs. It became a favorite, but I never knew why until that day in the museum gallery.

"She's his bright spot," I said to Susan, who was standing nearby. "He really loved her. He chose her. And, he only liked painting *her*. He never painted his second wife quite like this. Can't you feel his passion for Camille?" I felt mine ignite.

However, it was not the painting's composition and technique that grabbed me; I was trying to imagine the circumstances under which *The Red Kerchief* was originally created. Caught up in their emotion, I wanted what they had. Maybe next time I could get love right. I stepped closer to the painting and to understanding why my own marriage ended. I was not the name Joe called through garden doors. I never charmed him with a coy turn of my head. To him, I was a nameless, faceless blob in the crowd.

*   *   *

Walking inside Uncle Sam's that first time thirty years earlier was like entering the belly of a clown. It was dark and close. Patches of blinking colors quilted the dance floor. A spinning mirror ball threw specks of light onto distorted, inebriated faces, giving them a surreal, garish quality. Laughter burst from cells of people here and there, suddenly roaring and then quieting again. People wore shiny, sparkly and sequined clothing proportionately too small for their bodies, with wedges and boots that were too large. It was a Fellini-esque, three-ring-circus of a place. And despite my lack of sophistication, visiting a bar with the name blinking in red-white-and-blue neon atop the warehouse building should have been a clue that anything I found inside was the antithesis of romance.

Uncle Sam's was dozens of miles from my hometown of Roseville. It might as well have been a million miles from the lifestyle I knew. Married too early at eighteen, I traded bar-hopping for dish-washing early on. Now divorced at only twenty-one, my co-workers (*aka* The Girls at the Office) insisted I catch up for lost time drinking and dancing. There was round-heels Rhonda, a tall redhead who dressed in a form-fitting dress, tall heels and a trench coat like she just stepped out of a foreign film. Rhonda pretended to be particular about the men she picked up. There was Debbie, whose hard athletic body looked ready for a game of tennis or some such activity with bouncing balls. Kat was nicknamed from Kathleen because she was skinny, with feline movements, and wore black horn-rimmed glasses that made her look smart and film-noir distant. As the disco novice, I wore my backyard barbecue get-up, striped Hang Ten tee-shirt and white pants. My ordinariness stood out in the sea of halter tops and four-inch heels.

At Uncle Sam's, "looking for love in an all the wrong places" was *apropos*. Misplaced affection was something they wrote songs about; it was normal as apple pie, pina coladas in January, birth control packets in purses and one-night stands. "Clubbing" took the Neanderthal approach to dating, which was not unlike being hit over the head and dragged off to a cave. The primitive ritual began with men coaxing women to the strobe-lighted, high-decibel music. "Me . . . you . . . dance?" Percussion combined with musky pheromones was the 1970s aphrodisiac. Couples arrived with the mating glint in their eyes and left moments after meeting. Hollywood started reflecting this newfangled and hygienically dangerous phenomenon; boy meets girl in one scene and in the very next, clothing lays strewn about a bedroom and they're smoking a post-coital cigarette.

"Love loving you" lyrics moaned from speakers like the uncontrollable sounds of an orgasm. For Canadians such as Joe from nearby Windsor, Ontario, Uncle Sam's biggest draw was the wild American women and the hard-driving Motor City tunes—a musical cocktail of Motown, funk, and a dash of Bob Seger rock. The single woman's anthem "I Will Survive" screamed from the speakers many times throughout the evening. Lights flashed golden, cobalt and magenta, and they bounced off the disco-ball and checkered our squirming bodies.

I knew nothing of Monet that first night with Joe. And in this convulsive setting, there was definitely no lush, rolling Impressionistic valley into which we might venture and set out a blanket, bread and wine, finishing with a dessert-kiss so passionate that it pulled us down to the earth like gravity. The erotic never-ending cycle of reaping and sowing, give and take, dawn and nightfall, would never be found at a place like Uncle Sam's. Ours was a different dance. We only pretended to respond to one another . . . shake this and that "thang." No rainbows or puffy white clouds dotted a baby-blue Monet sky. It remained eerily midnight. Brightness might have revealed how animalistic we had all become. Club owners didn't want to scare us with our own inner demons; they only wanted a dark place for us to chase our desires into filthy corners, away from daylight and truth. I had joined the vampires.

With a swagger in his gait and twisted-up Elvis lip, half-inebriated Joe approached me, holding a long-neck brown bottle and wearing a faux-silk polyester shirt. He was a classic Sexy Seventies prince, but I was no disco diva. Mini-skirts were out because of my dimpled knees. My hair wasn't sprayed feathered and big; it was flat and smooth. I didn't have the money to buy club clothes.

A divorcee at twenty-one, I was not proud of this demerit on my relationship resume either. My demeanor showed my shame as Joe came closer. My shoulders slumped forward as if protecting my heart with my chest cavity and turning my back to more hurt. I often escaped into a daze that night, thinking about the viper of a woman who professed to be a friend, but slept with my ex-husband. She told me about their affair in the same tone as if telling me there was mustard on my chin. Sitting there among the strange lights and gyrating strangers, I still felt the phantom sting of discovering a long strand of her wavy, auburn hair in our bed.

Outwardly, my family supported me, but they were secretly ashamed. They talked to friends about my "unfortunate breakup" like it was a life-threatening car crash and I was lucky to have survived. I wore this double-shame, theirs and my own, like a boulder on the back of my neck.

Dancing might help me throw off the nagging helplessness that I could not change my past. I still didn't understand the work of marriage, but neither were my eyes wide open with childish wonder. My gaze had sharpened to that of a predator doing whatever it took to survive, such as accepting my hated office job at a plastics company. The job left me unfulfilled with its mind-numbing chores of typing, journalizing, and filing invoices for millions of plastic parts.

Joe did not see me across the crowded room, a beacon of beauty and light, as Claude Monet had seen Camille in *The Red Kerchief.* My future husband snaked his way through the pulsating bodies, looking for the loneliest and most defeated girl among them. I was a non-dancing fish out of the throbbing waters on the dance floor. When co-workers left me alone at the table so they could dance with their catches of the night, it must have been clear I needed someone.

"Anyone sitting here?"

Joe knew there was not. I motioned him to join me.

"What are you drinking?"

"Seven-Up. It's boring, I know."

"Not at all. That's exactly what I'm drinking." He stowed his beer bottle on an empty table nearby.

"I've never been here before," I said, looking around and acting as if I'd just arrived from another galaxy. This admission, plus the fact that I had dressed for a picnic and acted like a settled housewife, actually might have attracted him. Maybe I wasn't as likely to have a disease. Crabs was the popular STD during the summer of 1977. The Girls at the Office talked about it as casually as the sex they had to cause it.

"Me either. My first time too," he said, as if intrigued by my naivety. Marriage made me somehow pure again because at least I had chronically been with the same man. I probably was safer than the eye-fluttering cuties decorating the bar like butterflies on a bush. "You don't get out much, do you?" he said, watching me try to get the waitress's attention. "Here, let me." He motioned like he was calling a cab, and her young but seasoned body came running. He paid for two Seven-Ups and left the same amount for a tip. The waitress wiggled away, and he watched like a thirsty man imagining an oasis.

I have always wondered about a God who created some women who look and move that way and then others of us who do not.

When there was no conversation, sexual tension grew between us. We simply beat our heads and bodies to the rhythm to fill in the lulls. "What kind of music do you like?" he finally asked.

"The Bee Gees are pretty good," I said, figuring the disc jockey knew what he was doing. Something by the Brothers Gibb began nearly every dance set.

"They're my favorite, too," he said with an over-the-top optimism that suggested, *We've got so much in common already; we should probably sleep together as soon as possible.*

I smiled, not knowing how to respond. Meantime, I wanted to tell him that I was divorced, tainted goods. *You don't want me. I've been used and cast aside.*

Joe saw my sadness and countered it by making me laugh. "See that guy dancing over there? He looks like a drunken peacock, sticking his chest out, moving his head like this." Joe demonstrated from his bar stool like a stoned rooster. "And his feet don't even move."

"Oh, yeah. Well, I'm looking at that girl over there. Her straps are going to break any minute and those things are going to fall out onto the table." How quickly we became blatant and physical.

Club patrons were probably watching us too. Our dancing technique (two steps to the left, snap-snap, two steps to the right, snap-snap, and so on) was not John Travolta sassy and cool. But we no longer cared. We became a dancing unit, over-stimulated by the surroundings and under-concerned about anything else. Inhibitions melted. Monet, in his early caricature days, could not have sketched a more cartoon-like scene. Joe's arms and legs moved a second off the beat, and he wore a frozen smile like a maniacal disco jester in a fake-silk shirt. As for me, when the un-colas turned to rum and real cola, I decided that throwing my arms in the air this way and that way would enhance the hoochie coochie of my low-wagging hips. It looked like I either wanted sex or needed a comfortable chair to sit down.

Our meeting was not Kismet, nothing ethereal or magic. There was only banging music and danceable licks like KC's "I'm Your Boogie Man" and ABBA's "Dancing Queen." Diana Ross's "Upside Down" was the tune that finally tempted us to our feet. (Not exactly the kind of song we would tell our grandchildren about.) There were no roses or jasmine. No pretty Paris summer night. We generated heat on the dance floor, followed by cool drinks and more hot breath on each other's ears as we yelled above the din.

After hours of drinking-dancing and dancing-drinking, the unkind lights sparked on with the sizzle of flash bulbs, instantly killing the music. My ears rang like tiny tuning forks trying to recalibrate to the too-sudden, too-sane silence. The disc jockey walked away and puffed a cigarette like it was the nourishment he needed to get himself home at 2:00 a.m. Smoke drizzled gray, and overhead fluorescence blotched our skin yellow with reality.

We stood stunned for a minute before realizing the silence was our cue to flee outside, back to the darkness.

"Meet me here again next week?" Joe said, once we hit the fall air outside.

"Sure," I said, still reeling from the party so abruptly shut down.

"Oh, I forgot. Can I get your number?"

My sensible side had been on-hold for several hours, so what were a few more minutes? Those few minutes altered my future. I didn't want to let go. Joe picked me out of the girl-filled crowd. He watched me dance half the night. Now he wanted to call me. Flattered to submission, I assured "Don't worry" while ferociously digging through my purse. "I've got some paper and a pen somewhere."

I had not yet learned how to do aloof. As Joe waited, holding up the brick wall outside Uncle Sam's, I rapidly scribbled, hoping he wouldn't leave before I got everything down legibly, so he couldn't mistake a three for an eight or anything else that might cause him to not call me. "Here," I sighed. "So, I'll see you next week?"

I read his satisfied pirate-smile as mischief, the equitable kind we might get into next time. He lightly kissed me, the promise sealed, and he touched my cheek to complete the spell.

Back in my car, I turned on the radio. I needed a slight fix of rock music to take me back to that wonderful loose, lost feeling. I turned it off when Joe squealed out of the parking lot. I couldn't be sure whether he was angry that things only went so far or was simply eager to see me again. I opted to believe the latter.

*   *   *

That wintry day in 2009, as I stood in approximately the same vantage to view *The Red Kerchief* as Monet once had, I realized our views of romance were quite different. Looking at his painting in the museum thirty years after Joe's and my first meeting, I could now see Claude's deep desire for Camille. He wanted her, always had. As for me, I had recently remarried for the third time. I thought that nearly fourteen years alone was long enough to know what I wanted. Now, I wondered what brush I would use to depict this new relationship into something beautiful and worth keeping.

I no longer saw myself as a poor-man's jewelry box ballerina, stunned and frozen by the flash of a disco ball. But how could I be sure I hadn't merely traded a couple of letters in going from Joe to my new husband Tom?

"That's what I need," I told Susan, "a red scarf."

She stared hard at the painting trying to make the connection. She mentioned something about the gift shop possibly having one. I could not explain. I only knew my new marriage's success was not only dependent upon me, but recognizing the forces of love outside my control.

My new husband Tom had once sent me red roses in a ruby colored vase . . . stop-sign colors to get my attention. Now that they had faded and gone, would I continue to be the name he whispered in his sleep?

Chapter 4

Fruitful Thoughts

*J*oe and I never talked about having kids. We were on the road to Yuppie-ville, a place in America's history that was increasingly sexual yet put family second. The plan was to have a 2.5-car garage first, and then 2.5 children might follow. Sure, there were those early steamy window sessions in the back seat of his Monte Carlo, our hands and legs recklessly wrapped around each other. But breathless panting that "I want to have your baby" probably did not count as family planning.

Enter my mother-in-law. One late spring afternoon, Mum asked me to walk with her before dinner. I thought she wanted to escape the heat of the bubbling pots, one of them brimming with enough potatoes to feed twenty people and sputtering like it might lift off into space. We walked to the farthest corner of the one-acre yard, where pear and apple trees sprouted the first signs of fruit. A week earlier, the copious green marbles peeking from under lime leaves might have been missed, but now they blushed with burgundy. Mum opened her hand to display a fruitful cluster.

"They're so cute," I said, stroking their smooth roundness.

She dropped the fruit, then hung her folded hands below her navel the way a nun does before she delivers a scolding speech to a child. I recognized the posturing from catechism, where authority figures dressed in black-and-white looked us underlings square in the eyes. Next she would raise her chin to elevate her ideas above mine. Whatever issue she wanted to discuss, I was on the wrong end of it.

Mum went far beyond garden parables. She aimed straight for my Infertile Myrtle jugular. "You know, Marie, you ought to start thinking about having a baby," she said. "Joe's almost finished with school now. It's time."

My head tilted to adjust the picture of her telling me when to start a family. Hadn't she heard? It was a different era. Different economics. Birth control.

"You've been alone long enough," she said, as if our marriage was invalid without a child. She herself began a family nine months to the second after her honeymoon, which definitely trumped our two years sans infant.

She couldn't know how much the simple word "alone" hurt me. She might as well have said, "You're destined to wander the planet a lonely wretch, you whore." An only child for the first nine years of my life, my sister's birth had been a hallmark. Too small and helpless to be my playmate right away, Susan was still living, adorable proof that I was no longer "only."

Even one of my earliest memories involved role-playing that I was mother to six children. The number is significant only because it indicated the amount of available cubby spaces created between the two-by-fours that made up the skeleton of my childhood home's garage walls. I might have opted for more kids, but six slots equaled six babies. (Family planning was so much easier then.)

In the wall's recesses, where there were no garden tools or car paraphernalia, I laid my "babies" to nap beneath their respective numbers #1-6 written in chalk on the tar-paper lining. Then, leaving them to nap, I ran barefoot through soft green grass for the rest of the afternoon. Looking up, I saw the powdery blue sky, a backdrop to my own mother's smiling face as she reached down into the laundry basket and then hung wet clothes on a line to dry as they flapped like sails in the wind. The sheets smelled fresh-air fragrant that night. I drifted into worriless dreams, one of my babies tucked under my arm and the future non-existent in my "everything is perfect" mind.

Now fate had arrived and presented itself in the form of my mother-in-law. No surreal play, just real life. In the coming months, and without provocation, Mum would take up my cause of becoming pregnant like she was the minister of her own pseudo-religion called The Church of Becoming a Real Woman. Fertility was the only way to achieve salvation *and her approval. She would become more in tune with my body's rhythm than her son. And she took every opportunity to place one of her squirming grandchildren in my lap, so I could test-drive being a mom.*

Heading back to the house from the garden that spring day, I saw Joe's sister "Jenner," who was so nicknamed from the way she pronounced Jennifer when she was young. She stood behind the wall of glass that overlooked the garden and waved us back inside the house.

Mum was wholly pleased as she gazed upon her daughter, belly round with Baby Boy #1 of the three boys she would eventually have. "Doesn't she have that glow? There's nothing else like it."

I always liked Jenner. And it was true; she was pregnancy at its best. With her still-slender body, silky black hair and creamy skin, she was lovelier than any flower in a Monet garden.

Chapter 5

Eden (c. 1982-86)

Sitting at the foot of our bed, I notice the room has lost its garden-like warmth. So, this is the temperature of reality, then, skin crawling gooseflesh? I glance up at the Monet print of The Parc Monceau, *and its whole perspective instantly changes along with my own. For years I have looked at that picture hanging in our bedroom and have seen only morning brightness bursting through a big, bushy tree. But as I contemplate making one of the biggest decisions of my life, I notice evening's butterscotch settling onto the branches. People depicted in the park are no longer welcoming a new day; they are taking advantage of final spurts of energy to finish pleasures requiring daylight. Soon, windows and shutters will close. People will rest and wait out the night's chill.*

*   *   *

Claude Monet and I entered the realm of parenthood in our late twenties, but the endings of our stories were quite different. Family bliss shattered for Monet when Camille died, and he was left with twelve-year-old Jean and one-year-old Michel. His paintings are like a photo album of the lovers' brief time together. He captures life's sweetness in *Poppies at Argenteuil*, as wife Camille and oldest son Jean stroll among the flowers. *A Corner of the Apartment* is like a premonition in oil and canvas; another version of Jean emerges from the recesses of a somber room, lush with plants and gold draperies, leaving his mother behind as a shadow in the corner. Eventually, in *The Artist's Garden at Vétheuil*, Monet's youngest son Michel stands small, motherless, among the terraced landscape overgrown with sunflowers. I imagine Monet wondered whether a doting father was enough for such a small boy.

Claude Monet. *The Artist's Garden at Vétheuil*. 1880. (Oil on canvas, 151.5 x 121) National Gallery of Art, Washington, D.C. Ailsa Mellon Bruce Collection, 1970.

Any joy Joe and I might have experienced having children was eclipsed by two miscarriages and loveless sex. Or, was it the other way around? Claude and Camille were not at the mercy of infertility. And I don't believe they faced passionless liaisons when conceiving their two children. For me, sex for procreation's sake ranked right up there with sex for money. I didn't feel like a prostitute exactly; those interludes might have at least been steamy and maybe fun. Doctor's visits, countless tests, procedures and charting my biological clock's temperature spikes made me feel sterile as the cold metal examination table I visited far too often.

"Infertile" and "barren" were words I did not want to hear, yet that's all I thought about every month for five years. No impressions of Monet's fertile fields and valleys for me . . . only tilled earth devoid of sprouts or greenery. Now I was like the vacant rows of toxic earth shown in old newsreels about the Dust Bowl during the Depression. Winds whipped up the dry silt and blew the withering hulls away. Nothing would grow in my worthless womb.

When we first tried, I had become pregnant briefly—for one month—and lost my first baby at home. Just disgustingly and despondently flushed away. It was a "nonviable pregnancy," and so began the parade of medical terms and procedures that would dictate my life throughout my twenties. "Excruciating pelvic pain" followed, as did a "laparoscopy" to discover "endometriosis," the reason for discomfort and infertility. "Major surgery" followed the "exploratory" to remove the "chocolate cysts" that diabolically penetrated the walls of my uterus, escaping and spilling into the rest of my body like an open packet of rancid seeds. Unchecked, the cysts could become "cancerous."

I lost my breath.

"Breathing is good," the doctor joked, "every few seconds, whether one needs to or not." This favorite saying was actually stitched onto a needlepoint canvas that was framed on his office's bathroom wall.

I might have thought it funny too, except sitting in his stark office, with only his black-and-white credentials to decorate the room, and maybe a struggling houseplant on his desk, the air was stagnant. I felt stifled, stuck in the universe's mud. Did he expect me to jump at the chance for surgery because I would have a "bikini cut"? I was only twenty-four.

Six months later, the doctor was my hero when the test strip again turned blue. Strike up a chorus of "At Last" by Etta James, whose voice swirled like lingering cigarette smoke. Joe and I were satisfied. He acted as if he'd done his job. And I was enveloped in "fairytales can come true" euphoria. I visited a maternity store with the best designer duds for stylish breeders. I bought a pregnant guppy, and within a couple weeks, the squiggling fry sparked neon blue and pink all over the tank. I was in Mother-to-be La-la-land.

Sometimes, mostly when I was alone, my mind turned to the tiny particulate inside me, a microbe that needed magnification to even be seen. Insignificant as a tummy flutter, my soon-to-be child was the biggest thing in my life. I'd already had many silent conversations with the fetus. I agreed to take care of myself, but it had to use its influence with the Great Creator to survive. That was the deal. Rubbing my already rounding stomach during these talks, I loved and knew its spirit. That's why I recognized when it was gone.

"We'll watch things carefully," the doctor assured. Watching wasn't saving. At five months, the connection between baby and me disappeared. The doctor palpated my abdomen and listened with a stethoscope. He didn't understand that it wasn't a twinge in my pelvis; my heart beat only for one now. "Nope, can't find a thing wrong. I think you're just worried. It's normal, especially since we've already lost one. We got rid of the endometriosis and now you should carry the baby just fine. This is the happiest I've been with the pregnancy so far."

The boundaries between "us," "you," and "me" blurred between doctor and patient. The next morning, when I called about blood spots growing larger and redder as we spoke, the cheer had left the doctor's voice. "Call the hospital, and I'll meet you there."

I called ahead to prepare to save my baby, but there was no need.

"Don't bother coming in yet," the hospital nurse warned. "It (the blood) will fill your shoes when it's time."

Too soon I understood, as the cool stickiness ran down my legs. I apologized to the ambulance attendant for ruining the starched white sheets. As I entered a pleasing Demerol haze, the red swirled to pink and then faded to no color at all. No cares, no problems. Under the influence of the drug, I calmed down and rationalized there were plenty of pregnant women in the world, so one less didn't matter. Why was I crying again?

When the on-call doctor thought he was out of earshot, he quietly told Joe, "It will happen when she lets go."

Despite grogginess, my ears were hypersensitive and heard elephant footsteps leaving the room. "It" meant nonviable baby. "It" was a lump of hopes and dreams that had to be purged in a most grotesque way. A quiver ran through me as resignation set in and the baby gushed out. The doctor was right; when I lost the ability to care, It lost the ability to hang on. Suddenly, there were three of us in the room: the pacing nurse, the incomplete baby and me.

The sedative began erasing any memory of why I'd come to the hospital in the first place, and I stared at the ceiling. The pure whiteness enveloped my body, and I floated in the palm of a cool, soft hand. Call it Divine Providence, but something beyond the narcotics comforted me to sleep . . . until the nurse shook me back to consciousness.

"Quick, what's your religion?" she said, and the trembling nurse blessed the almost person. It looked like a baby, a teeny-tiny one, only without animation or that healthy pinkish hue.

The night I came home, I grieved my loss through a seal mother's plight featured in a TV nature documentary. "Don't turn it off," I yelled at Joe.

"Why do you want to watch this depressing stuff?" He seemed horrified that tears still burned my eyes and wet my pillow. He thought I had cried enough, and my soggy state annoyed him.

"I don't know," I said. But I lied. The truth was I immediately recognized the seal's forlorn moaning. The narrator explained how she had seen her cub's lifeless carcass with her own black eyes, and now searched for a replacement calf. Luckier seal mothers, who still had their babies, protected and coveted offspring from her envious glare. The filmmaker cut to an aerial view of the entire herd sitting on an outcropping near the ocean. Numerous seal mothers had experienced the same loss during breeding season. We all searched for something to hold and croaked our hurt.

I don't know how the seal dads handled it, but Joe paced the hallway outside our bedroom door. He would occasionally sit on the edge of the bed and hold me, but barely long enough to lift me up, then he'd let go and return to pacing and banging cupboards and slamming doors. Did this white noise help him to cope?

"Come to bed" was all I could offer, still numb from drugs and exhausted from plummeting hormones. No wonder he didn't want to return. What had happened in that bed in the course of twenty-four hours—waking to stained sheets, lying there waiting as the nurse directed and now returning infertile once again—had changed the tenor of the room and of our lives.

For months, I wore only black, a colorless color I'd never worn before. I found myself curious about everybody else's children. I searched their little faces for a snub nose or inquisitive eyes that might have been my son's. Though the doctor never told me, I knew it was a boy. A dream told me so:

> I enter an elevator. As the door begins to close, a slight but surly man comes aboard, making the tiny room even more claustrophobic. He carries a basket with a cloth over it. Though I can't see them, two baby boys are inside . . . alive, not dead. The agitated man wears a brown 1940's suit and a matching fedora. He devilishly looks up from under his hat brim and says, "You know they never belonged to you, right? They never were yours. You know that," he keeps repeating as if I have to agree and let him take my sons, or he won't leave me alone. I sadly nod yes.

*   *   *

A short time later, Joe and I left our sad small apartment for a fixer-upper home. Scraping wallpaper, painting walls, and cleaning away forty years of the previous owners' grime kept me too busy to grieve. We dispassionately fought about what color beige the kitchen tile should be. I focused my attention on creating a retreat in our bedroom, and *The Parc Monceau* became the room's centerpiece; its dawn-breaking theme the perfect optimistic start to every new day.

We never discussed the child that never was. In fact, Joe would wait five years to ask the soul-crushing question, "Don't you think it's time to have a baby? All my friends seem to have kids, and we don't."

I wondered whether his friends had awoken in a hospital bed to find they were barren again? Had their hormones nose-dived to the point that everything went pitch-black? I was vehement he should re-think his reasons for wanting a family. There had to be a better reason than keeping up with the 2.5 children the Joneses had. "Now you're interested," I shouted, letting loose a firestorm of rage. "I've finally given up, told myself it's not going to happen, and now you're ready. Where have you been?"

Two people can be physically together, at least in proximity, and yet each remains wholly alone.

Ultimately, we would try again, with a new sense of determination and a new doctor. The fertility specialist performed tests on both of us, and his assessment surprised me. "Do you really think you're ready?" From the start, it was clear he was not giving us a pep talk. If anything, it was a "think seriously about injecting potentially lethal chemicals into your system" discussion. "If we start giving you (hormone) injections, there's more to consider than whether we can make a baby."

There was? Finally, empathy. And I longed to know more. *Yes, tell me,* I thought. *Explain to me beyond how it's my job, how I'm supposed to be flexible and want to give of myself and my body, and how I'm not a real woman unless I can do what seems impossible. Yes, tell me, Great Helper to the Great Creator, what is the big secret to making new life?*

"You are high risk," he continued with common-sense not commonly found in medical professionals. "You've already had two miscarriages. And now that it's five years later, it could be even more difficult. Even if you do get pregnant, there's a good chance you might not carry to term."

Truth was an aspect of fertility treatment I had not considered. I was looking for a miracle, but miracle worker was not a title among my new doctor's credentials. He was a certifiable realist. "There's also the emotional and psychological aspect. It might not work. It could cost tens of thousands of dollars. How many times and how hard are you willing to try?"

He posed too many questions. Where was the magic pill that would make the child grow inside me like a beanstalk? Maybe there was a posture we hadn't tried. Or perhaps there was a mixture of herbs I could crush into a paste and spread onto a cracker.

Burst ovaries, cancer, blood clots and becoming a hairier woman . . . these were only a few of the dangers I read to Joe from a list of side-effects for the strong drugs I considered injecting daily. These contra-contraception talks were never easy with Joe; after all, it was my job to worry about pregnancy (and my fault we had not succeeded). The pharmaceutical pamphlets left him speechless. Maybe a word would have been nice. A question?

If my life had been a romance film, this would have been the point at which the leading man threw his arms around the leading lady and said, "Everything will be okay, and I'll be there for you," or "I want what you want, Babe."

But filmmakers rarely portray the authentic Eden of men and women.

Joe rose and left the spot on the couch where he had been sitting next to me. "Do whatever you want." He dismissively waved his hand. Dismissed from what? From baby-making duties? From our marriage?

✴   ✴   ✴

I escape to my refurbished room to lick my fresh infertility wounds. The 36"-by-24" print of The Parc Monceau *that hangs over our bed is finished with a pale blue frame to expand the softness of the sky. I don't remember choosing the frame for that reason, but it works. The comforter's floral pattern in soft pinks, periwinkle, white, and various greens makes Monet's flowering trees and bushes pop with vitality. A vase of similarly tinged silks on the dresser adds yet another dimension. These touches bring the Monet park garden to 3D life, only I notice for the first time that it's later in the day now. I am gratefully drawn into the soothing scene even more.*

I am waiting for Joe to join me here. Maybe, in a last-ditch gesture of love, he will throw me on the bed and say, "Forget the drugs and doctors. Let's just do it."

When he doesn't come to my bedroom retreat, I take comfort from classical music and The Parc Monceau. *Someone tinkles the keys to a Mozart piece, and it sounds like a wind chime. I had gazed at this idyllic scene often during the past five years, but I never noticed how much it actually shows life's mutability. There's a precise moment when a shift in perspective occurs like a shift in the sunlight. I only ever imagined life and hope, when, in reality, death and powerful eternity challenged people every day. Now I wonder who I think I am to expect more than a fleeting moment in the park.*

I lost innocence and a belief in magic that day, but found a new understanding about grace. In Monet's *The Parc Monceau*, I saw nature and its many-colored options in a brand-new light. Whether Monet depicted a honey-colored sunset or lemon-sun morning, both are extraordinary. It's not always birth and joy or death and sadness. One can also be re-born right here and now.

A year later I saw the doctor for my annual girlie physical. He surprised me by shaking my hand to show approval of my final decision to forego dangerous infertility treatments.

"Good choice," he said. "Now get on with your life."

Chapter 6

Loneliness Is . . .

Finding Out From Someone Else

My mother used to say that the only person I had to answer to was the person staring back in the mirror. One warm fall day in 1995, as I dressed for a court date to finalize a divorce from Joe, my reflection appeared fallen, sunken . . . transformed into someone who had the wind knocked out of her. At thirty-nine, I had a few creases starring the corners of my eyes. A few belligerent gray hairs sprung out here and there. Aloneness, however, cannot be cured by make-up or auburn dye.

The first epiphany about my solitariness struck the summer before I filed for divorce. I was in a store parking lot exiting my car when I felt dizzy. I gripped the door handle. With the car's air-conditioning now turned off, the humidity worsened flu-like symptoms. Was I sweating from the heat or from the intermittent waves of body temperature that rose and fell as the virus attacked? The curb seemed miles away, and walking there seemed impossible. If I did pass out before I got there, or got hit by a car, police would never have known who to call. It was the pre-cell-phone era, and they would not have found Joe at home or work. He had gone to some nebulous Somewhere for business. He would eventually contact me to be sure I was alone. He'd be jealous if I was out with a friend.

My driver's license would keep me from being a Jane Doe. But if I fainted right then, who would have signed the medical forms or approved a life-saving procedure? Joe isolated us from friends and family. They were called for holidays and weekends, but they were not involved in our secretive daily lives. Behind the domestic scenery of our presumed togetherness, there was a cavernous backstage room filled with nothingness.

Now, a year after my lonely epiphany, as I got myself dressed and ready for the final divorce proceedings, I could not help but notice my dull eyes, all the life and shimmer sucked right out. I wondered what still mattered to me, now that I was soon to be divorced from Husband #2. Who was I, if not a wife? Not a mother. Even my copywriting job was in jeopardy.

The look on my face reminded me of a late November day when rain has finally knocked down all the leaves. Total defoliation would occur with a final storm. My blank visage stared back at me.

Joe's affair represented only one of many tumbling down lies. His ex-boss Maureen validated my suspicions when she called a month after the divorce was finalized. She was his ex-boss by then, just like I was now his ex-wife. But she didn't call to commiserate. Her company was suing Joe, and because he and I were no longer married, she wondered if I would testify against him.

Maureen told me how the Other Woman had moved to Michigan. From where, I don't know. (Shock doesn't facilitate asking the right questions.) She said the lovers had spent documented time together. They bought a house nearby, about twenty minutes from our marital home. With the cool detachment of a teller giving me a bank balance, Joe's ex-boss explained how a private investigator watched my husband's every move for many months. "They spent time together in a mountain lodge," she continued, and the turning page of the investigator's report crackled through the phone, "during the last week of July."

My already splintered psyche took another hit. I felt violated that someone else knew more about Joe's activities than I did. Had the investigator been watching me, too? I imagined a dossier brimming with pictures of me dressed in a bathrobe as I took trash cans to the curb.

Maureen's revelation about Joe's travels with another woman was not truly news. Our Visa bill included a $90 charge for a leather purse bought in Colorado that never materialized as a gift for me. I cancelled the credit card. He never knew until one night a restaurant refused his plastic, and afterward he came through the door barking his embarrassment. He *never considered mine as I explained to the bank that I did not intend to accessorize another woman. But according to Maureen, there was a new twist: Joe had been passing off the woman as his wife while doing business on the West Coast.*

As a near-stranger told me about the secret life of the man I lived with for sixteen years and allegations of white-collar crime, I grew pale. Now, his behavior made sense. The deed he wanted to put in my name. The threats that his ex-boss was going to "get what she deserves." The phone calls behind closed doors. The constant need to leave the house for short bursts of time.

Bad Loving

A month before I filed for divorce, Joe and I had a quick, pointless liaison in Chicago. Nothing sexy about it. Fast and rudimentary. Dogs rutting in season had a better time. He heaved himself off with a final exhale, and I became the vacant vessel. No better than a whore and no more gratified. The sound of trousers whooshing back on and the clank of fastening his belt marked the end. My heartbeat was not melodic, but plodding; not primal, but the blip on a monitor to let me know I was still alive.

He grumbled, "This stupid zipper" and "Where the fuck are my shoes?" I couldn't imagine where he was going. Somewhere away from me, maybe. We had dinner plans—a nighttime cruise along Lake Michigan. But it was only 3:00 in the afternoon. We would spend the evening staring blankly beyond each other as we ate. The skyline would capture our gaze-less stares.

Through an open window, the hot August afternoon blew its hot breath on me. I limply fell back to the couch, where I had the most anticlimactic and oddly banal sex of my life. As I listened to the sounds of the city, everything seemed strange. Sex that made one want to cry, wasn't that reserved for rape? This was consensual. Wifely. Husbandly. My romantic notions dashed completely, I wondered whether I was strong enough to rebuild a new person from the fragments lying on the sofa in a downtown Chicago hotel room.

Being Afraid of the Dark

I remember one particularly fearful night just days before my leaving. Men's deep voices penetrated the walls from the living room into my bedroom. It was 1:00 a.m., and I pretended to get a middle-of-the-night glass of water, necessitating me to walk past the very room where several foreign-speaking strangers suddenly clammed up and fake-smiled. (I could hear thick Slovak-sounding accents as I walked down the hall.) Their eyes and bodies froze like predators waiting to pounce, as if I wouldn't notice them if they only stayed very still. My hand shook as I casually poured orange juice, and then I hurried by them again, softly making apologies for interrupting them. Their odd stares stiffened my spine. Closing my bedroom door for privacy felt futile without a lock on it.

One of these mysterious and suddenly close-mouthed men was my husband. He had agreed to sleep in a room down the hall after I filed for divorce, but most nights like these with his increasingly bizarre behavior after-hours, I worried he could hear my rabbit's heartbeat as I lay wide-awake, staring at the dark ceiling.

Claude Monet. *Camille Monet on her Deathbed (Camille Sur Son Lit De Mort).* 1879. (Oil on canvas, 90 x 68 cm). Musée d'Orsay, Paris. Gift of Mrs. Katia Granoff for museum Jeu de Paume, 1963.

Chapter 7

Adieu (c. 1998)

*A*t first glance, Claude Monet's *painting* Camille Monet on Her Deathbed *appears to be one of the most morbid scenes ever captured by an Impressionist painter. Delicate brush strokes seem to reflect Camille's final seconds and Monet's waning energy after the ordeal of her passing. Muted colors feathered onto the canvas do not disturb her sleep. Her silence fills the room, not even a puff of air left to exit taut lips. Monet applies gauzy light over her head and torso. Is that a final bouquet in the cold, unmoving grip of her fingers?*

I imagine Monet's hands are not steady enough to make exacting drips and dabs, especially to create real-looking blossoms. Why bother now, anyway? Let the blooms succumb to weeds. Rip off their gaudy heads or bake them dry in the sun. Camille's lifeless face becomes mannequin-like, hidden by rays of what appears to be first-morning light pouring through an unseen window like cool, pale milk. Yet it is the utmost reality. She will never hear birds chirp again or see a sunset. Her awakened life is over. Monet's begins anew.

Camille Monet on Her Deathbed *does not capture the backstage drama of ballet dancers whose candle-lit faces are full of emotion, as in a Degas scene. Youthful lightness had been extinguished for Camille and Claude. It also is not a canvas brimming with rosy-cheeked couples dancing at an outdoor party, like a Renoir. Vitality's rouge has rushed from Camille's face. The painting has none of the harsh edges of a*

Cézanne, whose skilled knife created crayon-colorful human figures and landscapes. Monet's surety has left him. Hues become blended and muted, misty dawn or dusk at the brink of nightfall.

Monet recreated the death mask amazingly well in *Camille Monet on Her Deathbed.* After watching the last breath leave my father, I can attest to its authenticity. I was surprised at how quickly the skin of my father's face lost its plumpness, how the final breath left the nostrils flat, and how the expression no longer animated the mouth, no more signs of a smile or a frown. Dad deflated like a balloon the split-second his spirit departed.

Seeing Madame Monet in the same supine position confirmed it; a final good-bye is inevitable in every relationship. I was drawn to the finality of *Camille Monet on Her Deathbed*, the centerpiece of the 1998 University of Michigan Museum of Art exhibit in Ann Arbor. The exhibit brought to the campus a touch of winter in France with a collection of Monet paintings representing what could have been the dregs of life, unless the painter was Claude Monet. When he experienced disparaging events, he painted tragedy as part of life's imperfect beauty.

Shortly after, in *The Ice Floes,* he would depict in ghostly winter hues the sleepy town of Vétheuil, where Claude and Camille most recently had made their home before she died. The frigidity of bare branches reached up from the icy river into an unfeeling gray sky. Likewise, in *Sunset on the Seine in Winter,* the entire landscape seemed scorched from the frosty effects of the most unforgiving of seasons.

As Monet approached his fortieth birthday and mid-life crisis, it appeared twenty years of painting landscapes to hang over mantels in presumptuous parlors had taken its toll on his artistic sensibility. After Camille died, the work seemed to change. Monet's Haystack series of paintings began to reflect the varied effects of seasonal light and weather on simple piled-up wheat fronds in a farm field. It's the ordinary made exquisite. A few more years down the artistic road, he would move to Giverny to begin his forty-year odyssey into re-creating visages of the gardens he planted, culminating with larger-than-life, lily-pad-covered canvases stretching the length of his studio.

Claude Monet. *The Ice Floes (Les Glacons)*. 1880. (Oil on canvas, 97 x 150.5 cm.) Shelburne Museum, Shelburne, Vermont.

Meantime, some narrow-minded critics called him merely a "decorative painter." But, were frescoes in Greece and Pompeii fancy house paintings? Was the Sistine Chapel another ornate ceiling? More than filling a blank wall, or compensating for fading eyesight, I believe these water-garden paintings thrilled Monet's soul. A sensuous release. After Camille died, he began expressing life in split seconds. He found life's profundity in its fragility.

*   *   *

The day I knew it was over with Joe, I was in our new Jacuzzi bath, mesmerized by a miniature eight-by-ten version of Monet's water lilies hanging over the tub. He hadn't physically left the marriage, but he had emotionally shut off like a faucet. His usual few-day business trips became weekends and weeks away.

He took a nearly empty suitcase for a trip to Florida, and he returned with a full wardrobe of new shirts and shorts in freaky colors. The duffel brimmed with Ken-doll chic clothing in gold, tangerine, purple and patterns; gone were his usual conservative blues and grays and pinstripes. Apparently, each day away had required a new ensemble. At home his summer clothes usually consisted of holey tees and bleached-out shorts. When asked why he hadn't he taken some of the brand-new duds in his closet, he told me he wanted "something new."

I wondered if Miss Something New was pretty. Was she the kind who took cuts and stepped to the front of the line at the coffee shop because she wanted everyone to see her, as if she herself were on display in the pastry case? Maybe she was the strong athletic type, whose outdoor glow, perfectly chiseled teeth, and wild, free hair looked as if she had recently returned from hiking Mount McKinley, so physical and ready.

Did she think he cared? She would soon find out that he didn't have it in him. Oddly, whether she was the "flavor of the week" or a country club diva who might further his career, I almost wanted to warn her. Almost. Mostly, I wanted to read the eyes of the woman who dressed my husband in these foreign clothes. I was convinced she wanted me to know she was out there, waiting for him to return. So, she sent a message in tropical prints.

The pile of tainted garments remained unwashed on the day I left. It would have been like handling radium for me to sort through what he wore after they made love. I'd flinch at the touch of sand in his pockets, leftovers from where they stretched out on the beach. Maybe I'd find a book of matches from the ocean-side restaurant where they toasted their final night together.

He dumped his suitcase and immediately left again. Had "a few things to do." To avoid the contaminated clothing, I took a cleansing soak. As the hot water swirled, my skin tingled with pinpricks of mistrust, suspicion, and shock. Soon I couldn't tell where the salted water ended and my tears began. Such red-hot baths had often hidden the flushed symptoms of a failing marriage, when anger made me a sharp, prickly hot burr the universe could not swallow.

Crying purged the disappointment. I was not living a passionate life; I wasn't living at all. I was no liar; yet I lied all the time by covering the bruises with long-sleeve shirts. Punches were frequently delivered in the car, to the point I made excuses to drive myself and meet him places. "Oh, I've got a few errands to run. I'll just take my car and meet you." But sometimes, trapped in the front seat a couple feet away from him, I might mention he ran a red light or how he came too close to another vehicle. "Stop, stop, stop," I'd yell, as my right foot staccato-pushed a phantom brake. He punched me so many times in the left arm that whenever I sensed his temper flare while driving, I automatically bent to the right to ready myself.

I pretended to be happy in front of people, diverting their attention with stories about our latest trip. Thankfully, we traveled a lot, though I wonder now what it might have been like traveling the English countryside with someone who was not angry because the roads were so narrow. I remember warning him we were too close to the rose-covered stone walls. I mentioned being able to smell the flowers because they were practically shoved up my nose as we drove by. When the hubcap got caught in the vines and popped off, I received a punch for my sarcastic fortune-telling. Sometimes, when recounting these stories, I'd overcompensate with nervous laughter. Or I might engage in silly, bubble-headed conversations to entertain. "Oh my *gawd,* let me tell you about the new restaurant we found that has beef ribs that look like they came from a dinosaur. You *have* to go."

Milking such inane conversations, I didn't dare lapse into talk about our real life. People didn't want to know what it was like to wake every day, wondering how to escape the "forever" promise I made. They didn't want to know how I feared happiness because something violent always followed to quash it. Flatness of affect protected me from pain and worry. It was better that way.

Joe always said, "No expectations, no disappointments." In his mind, emotional flat-lining was a nice place to be.

The extra-deep tub was my cocoon. It covered me to the neck like a blanket or a hug. Joe didn't like touching or being touched, at least by me. He complained that it "tickled" or "hurt." Reassuring squeezes around his neck were not welcome. He peeled away one arm and then the other, shaking his shoulders free. I suffered this rejection. But stewing in the bath that day, I refused to clean the new rags he had worn with her. Thinking about him lavishing attention on another woman, I squirmed down deeper. Only my mouth, nose and eyes stayed above water. The jets pulsated against my skin, jiggling my flesh and jarring emotions. Blankly gazing into the nebulous, shrunken water lilies hanging above the Jacuzzi, I couldn't admit it was over.

If it had been anybody else in the tub—a friend or family member—I would have told her there was no reason to live this way. Get out. Dry off. Leave. I would have taken her away from there, bought her lunch, and let her cry it out. Started the healing.

I suddenly remembered what the policeman had told me. "It always gets worse." Then he stopped himself from explaining all the eventualities. "Leave now," he warned, keeping something back that frightened even him too much to tell. Instead, he shook his head like he was disappointed in me.

Going to the police station was not my idea; the emergency room doctor who took the x-ray to rule out a broken clavicle said he had to report it. "I'd recommend you go straight to the police station when you leave here."

I stood just within the door at the police station, afraid to go all the way inside. That would make the abuse official, would put it on a permanent record and make it real.

The officer read my shame and softened his voice. "The sooner you leave, the sooner you can start your new life." It was like he was offering a child candy to come in off the streets. But I was not falling for it.

That night in the bathtub, I knew he had been right. Each time, the hitting escalated into harder, longer sessions, and Joe was more antagonistic. He would dare me to leave, but then block the door with his body. What might happen next time I was trapped inside? Plus, sleeping with him now meant sleeping with Her. I never suspected other women beyond flirting, but this time was different.

A few days before, when his friend Chaz asked where Joe had gone, I said, "He's in Florida meeting clients," as if it was normal for business meetings to last two full weeks, without a single phone call. Usually when he was gone, he called morning and night to check on me.

"You know what they say, Marie," Chaz said like a confidante. "The wife is always the last to know."

"Know what?" I said then. But once Joe was home, there was no refuting the new Floridian wardrobe he expected me to wash, no questions asked.

A righteous "no" unexpectedly rose up and eked out of my clenched jaw as the rest of me effortlessly floated in the water. I repeated it like a chant, each time more loudly—no, No, NO, as if exorcising demons back to where they came from.

A few days later, Joe once again raised an angry hand above my head, only this time I remained unafraid. I can't remember what started the argument. Nothing important. It never was. But in the bathtub that previous night, I had realized that my twenty-year search for something better yielded only violence and deception. I imagined him and her as a pair of sharks, sleeping side-by-side, wondering who would wake up and devour the other first.

I anticipated Joe's fist landing on my shoulder. Would I bend away as usual? Later, he might kiss the bruise and tell me he was sorry. He would say he was forced to do it. My transgression? Maybe it was the dirty laundry still piled up after his trip. Maybe it was such a bad day at work that he wanted to leap off the roof. He often called and threatened to do it, and I'd talk him down. Maybe we had something non-gourmet for dinner. I don't know what it was that made him mad, but much as I tried to swallow it, this time that still unfamiliar "no" rose again in my throat.

"What did you say?" He sounded surprised.

"Or go ahead," I coaxed in a voice I didn't recognize as my own. "It's up to you. But if you do, remember you have to sleep."

His eyes widened; his smile went blank. "What? I wasn't going to do anything." He was the child caught before breaking the vase. "So, what are you going to do, anyway?"

"If you ever touch me again," I promised, "I'll wait until you're asleep, and then I'll take a baseball bat to both your knees."

Joe had been a cross-country runner, and his knees were his weakest point. That made some sense. But I have always wondered why I chose a bat. We didn't own one. I didn't play ball. I never even spanked my dogs. Perhaps his lofted arm reminded me of someone ready to swing a bat over the plate. It was an equalizing image for me weighing in at 140 pounds and him at 230.

His raised arm and fist came down by his side, and my shoulders relaxed.

I made sure we were in a public place the next time we talked. I didn't trust him or even myself now. Actually saying, "I'm filing for divorce" sounded surreal, like something that wasn't possible.

"Not until I get my half," he shouted, defending his interest in our recently remodeled home's equity. He flung a stool across the coffee shop, his way of dotting the "i" of our discussion. His car screeched away.

I apologized to the cafe owner, thankful I'd driven myself. There was no going home now. That would have been like walking into a dragon's lair; he was already in a bad mood, and now I had pissed him off.

*   *   *

I was thirty-eight going on thirty-nine, about the same age as Monet when Camille departed. It's not exactly a fair comparison—the artist losing his wife to premature death and his career taking a nosedive at mid-life, and me losing my marriage to another woman and my job to down-sizing. Separation from the one person with whom Monet had shared his heart, bed and artistic impulses was quite different from the chasm of indifference that cleaved Joe and me apart.

I was flawed, the common denominator in two failed marriages. Still, I mourned the end of an eighteen-year relationship as if it were a death, the waking of a dream for elusive happiness. I closed off my soul like an unkempt room, where the emotions had to be tidied up before it could be opened up again. How had love turned to hate? Titillation turned to revulsion? Many questions had to be answered before I could commit again.

When I visited that Monet exhibit at the University of Michigan in 1998, for which *Camille Monet on her Deathbed* was the centerpiece, it was three years post-divorce. I was happily single. During this time, my mid-life portrait would have had no face, only the impression of one. My eyes would have been omitted because I still didn't know myself. There would have been no lips in this picture because I didn't recognize or speak truth anymore. To paint our strained marriage would have taken a coarse brush to create wide, long strokes of black, blue, and splotches of fiery orange.

Just as the paintings in the Ann Arbor exhibit portrayed Monet's winter phase, I had entered my Yellow Period. Life was nebulous; not strongly male or female. Neuter. I would not enter another relationship for nearly a decade. Love-blindness and ambition defeated me before. And the shame of being made a fool twice caused desire to wholly fade away. At first it was a cave-like, claustrophobic place to find myself. Similar to Monet's boorish patrons, who wanted lovely afternoon landscapes to fill their parlors, friends nagged me to accept all the clichés. "Find the silver lining." "Get back on the horse and ride." "Dawn always comes after the darkest part of night."

What about giving love-lost the credit it deserved, as Monet had done with his final painting of Camille? He could have painted the sunrise following Camille's death, signifying the moment at which his new life broke onto the horizon. Instead, he painted her in a somber way, an honest depiction of what horrific event hatched his new life that bleak morning. It helped him (and me) to remember what it's like to be jolted back to reality, despite Death's (or Divorce's) unwelcome visit. He captured that unique form of hunger—losing love and wanting it back—that cannot be satiated by anything but true emotion.

I now looked at my failed marriages as more than endings. They were thresholds to a new life. Whether good or bad, all relationships revolve full circle. Joe's and mine had seen its "forever."

As I left the university's exhibit hall, I couldn't help but feel that *Camille Monet on Her Deathbed* was not moribund. It was one of the most real and loving subjects Monet ever explored with a paintbrush. No one can know what Monet saw as he looked into the fading face of his Camille, except that some bright spot he'd previously known had extinguished. Maybe he would compensate for his loss in other ways, such as his second marriage, and in his later paintings (including the oversized water lilies series). Or maybe he remembered Camille's final morning every time he picked up a paintbrush. We'll never know. People who intersect our lives leave a lasting impression, no matter what the circumstances.

For me, the visage of Camille in her final moments reveals a message in oil-and-canvas code: every relationship ends.

Claude Monet. *Nympheas (Waterlilies)*. 1914-1915. (Oil on canvas, 160.5 x 180.5 cm.) Portland Art Museum, Portland, Oregon. Helen Thurston Ayer Fund.

Chapter 8

Beauty (c. 1995)

I needed a break from the November ugliness, and standing in front of Monet's water lilies at the Art Institute of Chicago reminds me of springtime. The canvas is larger than I imagined. And the bigger-than-nature lilies themselves are strewn asymmetrically a bit more on one side of the pond than the other. They are an amalgam of pinks, softly pale to crisp fuchsia, which taken together equal the nuances of a flower. After all, what bloom is absolutely one solid color throughout? Veins of darker shades carry water to the tips, which themselves are dipped in darker hues. Shadows titillate with an evocative melding of petals one into the other. Tender folds hide even more tender secrets.

The lilies splash up out of their languishing bath and aspire toward the sun. Is that a hint of pale yellow there on that petal, or softer ecru? Shimmers on the water are expressed in long liquid strokes. Sparkles are not slight, but bold as the light itself. The physicality of colorful movements does more than tell the story of light upon the watery segment of the artist's garden. His passion for nature's beauty expresses itself with each dab of pigment. I feel the fire of his spirit; his warmth radiates from the work, sparking my own enthusiasm.

Monet's passion leaps from the canvas, proving the existence of beauty. The lilies themselves float on a mosaic of strong staccato brush strokes that quickly capture nanoseconds of flickering light upon his Giverny water garden. Monet applies colors muted and bright, textures chunky and then smooth. Monet paints outside any frame . . . outside the limits of size, ideals or what was. Would I ever feel free enough (young enough) to color outside the lines again?

*   *   *

While married to Joe, I was more the garden diva type than a kitchen queen. Unfortunately, he liked to eat gourmet. While I could duplicate simple dishes like domestic potato salad, meat loaf or stuffed cabbage, my experience with true cuisine was lacking. Like Monet, I would escape all day into the garden patches that popped up all over the yard . . . planting, weeding, and relishing what grew. There, I was free. Conversely, the kitchen closed in on me, with the "big white hot thing" and the "big white cold thing" bullying me into lengthy preparation of dishes that instantly disappeared. It seemed like reverse creativity.

During the first month of my marriage to Joe, one night he cleared the kitchen table with one sweep of his arm, launching plates and shattering glasses. The reason was not clear to me. Maybe the macaroni and cheese was not good enough. Maybe I didn't season it like his mother. Maybe I said something insensitive. Did it make any difference? There was food dripping down the wall.

"Now clean it up," he roared, daring me to defy him the way a bull does when it taunts yet warns not to come any closer.

I wanted to flee, but his 200-pound, still-vibrating-with-anger frame stood before the door. Strangely, back then I figured he wanted me to stay. Now I know I should have left immediately and worried about his motives later. But I didn't. A few dustpans full of broken glass were dumped into the trash, the wall was washed, he kissed me, and normalcy returned to our married life.

Several months later, as I got off the elevator and began down the hall toward our apartment, the stink of parmesan cheese met me head-on. The closer I got to our door, the more pungent the stench. Joe had filled a pot with two jars of spaghetti sauce, an eight-ounce container of parmesan cheese, and two chopped raw veal cutlets. He let it simmer to a disgusting consistency and an odor strong enough to force a gag reflex.

Maybe he was trying to help. Why didn't I suggest we order a pizza? But no, I made a big deal of it, insulted him. "You don't dump everything in a pot," I insisted.

"What was I supposed to do?"

"How about use a recipe?" Thankfully, the rancid air had thinned enough, so I could now look directly into the red goop without my eyebrows melting away. "You've ruined the meat."

"We can still eat it," he said.

"Are you kidding me? I'm not eating that. How much parmesan did you put in there, anyway?" I laughed some more.

"The whole jar." He still did not know why that was wrong.

"No, no, no," I said, as if he were a child. "You have to bread and fry the meat. Layer it together with the sauce. Cover with grated cheese. Then bake it." I was still laughing. "You thought *this* was veal parmesan."

His whole body tensed up like a giant lump of muscle. I don't remember eating dinner that night, but I do recall cleaning up the smelly red slop splashed into the sink, and decorating the walls, counter and floor.

Because of these early kitchen debacles, I opted for gardening to express my domesticity, creating an indoor garden in our first apartment and asking a friend to make a window box for the balcony. Buttery squash blooms unwound every day during our first summer together.

I couldn't avoid the kitchen altogether, however. Before our final break-up, there was one final kitchen occurrence. It happened on one of many conflict-riddled days leading up to the divorce, when Joe threw $10-a-pound ground sirloin onto the floor, protesting, "I don't eat hamburger. And don't cook anything for me ever again."

It didn't matter that it had been steak a few minutes before it was freshly ground at the market. It was a hot September day. "I thought it would be fun," I weakly said, re-thinking why I thought we would suddenly have a good time together.

His foot smashed the package, squishing the blood-marbled mass out of the sides and onto white linoleum. He stared angrily into my eyes as if I had just tried to feed him worms. "I'm not eating this East Side crap." He made a door-slamming, wall-shaking exit.

"Go ahead. Maybe she'll make you a five-course meal. Good. Enjoy yourself, you son of a bitch," I shouted after him. This time I felt stupid for buying food for a man I was divorcing . . . one who was violent . . . and one I knew had another woman elsewhere. So much for amicable endings.

I never did like dealing with hungry people. I was never a waitress, and now cooking left a bad taste about relationships, too. A year after the divorce, I had a perfectly Dali moment that represented how we all look without our human masks as we hunger after our desires:

> *Walking through the video store this late November afternoon, I notice a box among the Halloween horror movies still on display. Pictured on the VHS cover is the head of a wolf-like creature baring its fangs. The skin is peeled from its muzzle and head, and the shininess of tissue below gives it that extra rawness, revealing what terrible animals we all can be under the skin. We threaten with our terrible teeth to get what we want. We snap at each other. We take. We demand what is ours. We move along in pursuit of the elusive More.*
>
> *I shudder at the realization this is what my ex-husband looks like behind incredibly blue eyes.*
>
> *Outside the video store, suburban Detroit mirrors my mood. The video-store door whooshes closed tight against freezing temperatures. The trees have finally changed to post-apocalyptic black and grey sticks against a colorless dusk sky. Once rosy, golden and flame-orange, the brown leaves are in the process of becoming earthy mulch. Smoke hangs in the skies, slowly exits chimneys and spews from car manifolds like gray-white cotton candy.*

Outside the video store, I shuddered, pulled up my collar and surveyed the coldness. I wanted something beautiful to counteract the hideousness of what people do to one another. A week later there was an article in the paper about the Monet exhibit. I ordered tickets for my sister Susan and myself on the red-eye to Chicago.

*   *   *

Susan and I both needed a break. She and her boyfriend had also come to an impasse in their relationship, and she felt her only choice was to let him down easy. "Your getting a divorce made me think, 'Why should I put up with it? I'm not even married to the guy.'"

I felt like anything but a glowing example of what a good partnership should be. Divorced twice. Failed as a wife. Never a mother. Allowed myself to be deceived. Our parents met in kindergarten and knew each other their whole lives. They had only ever loved each other. They had only ever been married to each other. They trusted each other. I had let them down.

My father liked to tell the story of deciding to marry my mother when he was only seven. "We were going on a field trip, and your mom's mother was driving. Even though the car was filled with girls, I said 'I want to go with her.'" Every time he re-told it, my father would point at my mother as if he was a pirate who finally found his treasure. "I knew I would marry her someday."

Whenever Dad told the story, Mom always returned a sassy smile, indicating it was weird that a second-grader would pick his future missus this way, and yet it was flattering because someone loved her so much that he would pursue her for the next ten years to make good on his promise. Now I was failing their legacy and failing as a big sister—a couple more negatives I could add to my repertoire of mistakes.

Once inside the Art Institute of Chicago, I knew the trip was what we both needed. Susan and I went straight to the Monet exhibit, beginning with *Garden at Sainte-Adresse*—a crisp garden scene, marked by a small group of people looking out to sea and viewing what seemed a fleet of ships. Red, white and blue popped off the canvas. We could practically hear the flags snap in the wind and smell the pollen from flowers rendered in the patriotic colors of France. Red details adorned the lady's gown. A white parasol reflected the bright sun. Even the whiskers on one man's face seem tactile. Susan's cheeks flushed pink and her eyes flashed blue at the artistry, and a new Monet devotee was born.

We lost ourselves as we separately meandered through the Monet maze, winding in and out of more than a dozen chambers that made up the exhibit.

Hours later, Susan and I met up again in one of the final rooms, where I had found *Nympheas* (*Waterlilies*) and couldn't tear myself away. Outside, Chicago was frosty cold; inside, the painting teemed with lusty new life and rebirth. Happy as an amoebae squiggling under the water's surface, and lingering much longer than the few minutes requested by the museum, I immersed myself in the painting and forgot responsibility, decisions, and judgments about being a two-time divorcee who couldn't cook.

Monet was nearly double my age, nearly eighty, when he painted with the expansiveness found in his water lilies series. He was old, but painted as if shouting through a megaphone. He no longer seemed to care what critics thought. And he wasn't stifled by his near-blindness or perfection. He loved color and nature and recreated it loudly, vividly. His way.

"Why are you crying? Is it making you sad?" Susan asked. She did not understand my unhappiness when I was looking at something so gorgeous. "This is one you really wanted to see, right?" Though never out of touch, she and I lost some of our sisterly closeness during my marriage, and it felt good to have it coming back. The magic of the lilies entranced her as well.

How could I explain? Should I? Or, should I let her experience it on her own? I could only hope she would feel what I did. I hoped she wanted the kind of life that fostered such free-ness, openness. Before that day, I always figured passion for living was doled out incrementally, like a paycheck. We only had so much giving stored in our hearts. Wasted on the wrong people—two ex-husbands, in my case—it was gone forever. Not renewable. It was the most awful and irreversible type of shame, wasting of love.

"I'm not really crying," I said. "It's just that he never gave up. He painted almost sixty years to reach this point." I emphasized "sixty" as if it were just not possible. "He was almost blind. Probably had arthritis. Maybe broke. But he didn't give up."

Tears rolled freely now to reveal that I wasn't done either.

Claude Monet. *The Japanese Footbridge and the Water Lily Pool, Giverny.* 1899. (Oil on canvas, 89.2 x 93.3 cm.) Philadelphia Museum of Art, Philadelphia, Pennsylvania. The Mr. and Mrs. Carroll S. Tyson, Jr. Collection, 1963.

Chapter 9

Coloring (c. 1997)

Ten bucks can change your life. When I bought a cheaply framed print of *The Japanese Footbridge*, I had no idea it would absorb me into a brand-new flow of life like the water running beneath it. It was discarded in the clearance room of a store where I found three rooms of furniture for under $1,000. Even the garish yellow sign and frame's fake gilding could not diminish the masterful layering of blues and greens. The print appeared darker than I had seen in books, colors muddy from reprinting. Claude Monet's unmistakable style remained.

"Are you getting rid of this?" I asked.

The clerk shrugged, taking the $10 bill I offered.

I renovated and furnished a small ranch home two years post-divorce. I steamed away wallpaper. I scrubbed bathroom tiles from gold back to yellow. I ripped up forty-year-old carpet stiff with dirt. I painted everything milky white, like a fresh page onto which I could write my new life. As a finishing touch, I hung *The Japanese Footbridge* in the middle of the living room wall.

The interior's new brightness aired out my soul, purifying my dusty, dark past. But like Monet, who eventually brought back the color to his canvas and his life, I needed to feel joy again. I was ready for a splash of color, but not for a new man. Yet along came Mr. Southern Gentleman, who threatened to disrupt my transition from hopeless to happy again.

He had gotten my name from a business card exchanged upon meeting at a mutual client's office. I was a freelance writer who crafted words to sell everything from flowers to the "fleet and fancy" Lincoln Mercury. The "Southern Gentleman," which is how he referred to himself often during our first conversation, represented a printing company. He mentioned he was looking for a writer now and then. That's how he initially sized me up, not for the too-soon discussion of my underpants situation which would ensue.

"Hi, it's Tony," he said with a Broadway ta-da quality.

"Tony?" I didn't have a friend named Tony.

"You remember me . . . the guy you met last week."

Still nothing, not a single memory bell.

"You offered me your card?"

Then I remembered . . . too many affectations, cat nervous and a touch pushy. A real salesman. I turned on my professional voice. "So, did you get the job?" I asked since his meeting had followed mine.

"Yeah, I did, but that's not why I'm calling."

"Oh," I said, disappointed that he was not offering more writing work to help pay for the costly home renovations. "So, *why* are you calling?"

"I think you're cute as a button."

An uncle or grandfather once said this to me, and I didn't like it when I was six or seven. I really hated it at forty. I remember thinking, *If he calls me Toots, I am not responsible for what I might say.* "Aw, that's nice of you."

"Are you dating anyone right now? I got the impression you were single, and I'd like to take you out sometime."

"I appreciate that. I'm really flattered," I said. "But I never mix business and pleasure." And that was that, or so I thought.

Then he really started his pitch. "You've obviously never dated a Southern Gentleman. I'll sweep you off your feet. Send you dozens of roses. You'd like that, wouldn't you?" He sighed as if already picturing our tryst in his lecherous mind.

He was starting to scare me. Plus, how could I explain the emotional safety I felt in my alone-ness? Instead, I used the excuse that my new house kept me far too busy. "I can't date right now. Not you. Not anybody." The excuses flowed like water. "I have never been a single home owner." "The grass needs cutting." "The house needs work." "I have bills to pay." "There's so much work, I just don't have time."

My potential stalker never asked, but I could tell my recent move only intrigued him. "R-e-e-ealy," he said like he was cornering me. Or maybe he sensed my enthusiasm and wanted to catch onto the caboose of the runaway train that had become my new life. He persisted. "Anyway, I think you're a real doll."

Now being compared to a Kewpie took me back fifty years to a time when my mother would have been called "doll," but my dad never dared. And then the clincher: "By the way, do you wear garters or pantyhose?"

"Pardon me?" I was ready to talk printing processes with him, not panties. "That's none of your business."

He either did not hear me or had become so engrossed in his own sexual fantasy, he couldn't stop himself. "Garters are so much sexier," he said, "like those actresses in the Forties and Fifties who showed some leg. Real hot. Would you wear those?"

In my mind, he had instantly gone from potential colleague to compulsive psychopath dreaming how he would undress me and, possibly, finish me off. "So, you like old movies?" I said, trying to keep it as superficial and PG as I could.

"Not really. I like when a girl dresses like a girl, that's all."

No innocent, idle chatter in this first phone call, only an attempt to get me aroused with talk about which under-things he liked most, including garters and hose, under-wire bras that closed in front, and silky, body-hugging slips worn as negligees.

I cringed. Forget the Forties; things had dramatically changed since the Seventies. Twenty years later, no plying me with dinner and a movie first? Men didn't get women inebriated anymore? That way, the tiny pieces of Lycra and lace he talked about fell off on their own. Oh, for the days of fifteen minutes of foreplay. He made me hot all right, but not for sex. I was furious. "I really have to go. I'm in the middle of something."

He acted like I should jump at the chance to have sex with him. "I thought you would want to go out. You are divorced, right?"

I suppose I could have pulled out my moth-eaten negligee from my previous marriage and gotten right back into the sexual saddle with Mr. Southern Gentleman. But creepiness oozed up my spine, an intuitive warning that nothing good could come of a relationship solely based on garter belts.

I didn't want to be labeled as a bitch throughout the Metro Detroit advertising community, which was a small, tight universe. I would likely run into him again, and as luck would have it, I eventually did. So I'm glad I didn't lambaste during this first phone conversation. "I'm sorry, I have to go now," was all I said. "Thanks for calling."

*　　*　　*

For several months, I forgot about the uninvited phone call and dug deep into home-decorating (like only a woman trying to hide tracks of her past can do). No compromises; everything in my home had to be re-done and re-surfaced to reflect me. To decorate my living-room-turned-reading-nook, I started with a solid-wood bookcase I practically stole for $20. The shelves held many friends: *The Great Gatsby,* my newest collection of Eastern philosophy and even an original copy of Margaret Mitchell's *Gone With the Wind.*

What happened next was pure Monet. *The Japanese Footbridge* framed print added a kick of color, but the room's overall blandness dwarfed the picture. I took the print with me to the local hardware store and purchased pints of summer sage, spring leaf green and terra cotta—all pastel shades of the darker tones found on Monet's palette for *The Japanese Footbridge.*

At home, I place the Monet print nearby for inspiration. Then I mask off one-inch around the accent wall's border. I carefully begin to sponge-paint using the least used shade, a peachy orange to complement the rich rust-colored plants edging the banks near the footbridge. Careful at first to dip in my sponge only enough to get the tip wet, soon my hand is covered in the pleasing goo of paint. I rapidly dab at the entire height and breadth of the featured wall, allowing enough white to pop through so it blends with the other three totally white walls.

I begin to understand the ecstasy of applying pigment where there once was none. The wall becomes my canvas. Grand movements mimic Monet himself as he covers his oversized water lilies canvases. Though it is the holiday season and cold outside, I break into a sweat. The physicality is exactly what I need. Repression unleashes.

If Monet had a CD player, he would have played Enya or something whimsically French like Carla Bruni for musical white-noise. I develop a rhythm and layering technique for applying the darker and then the lighter variants of green to further duplicate key elements in The Japanese Footbridge. *The moodier pastel green first, yes, to represent the leaves and stems of established plants. A brighter shade of vert follows in delicate spongy splotches, giving a sun-kissed effect to the new-leaf colors on my Monet-inspired wall. I touch up with peach to again pick up the russet undertones. I don't notice time passing. Then, Voila!*

The embellished wall brought the garden inside and created an ideal backdrop for the Monet print I re-hung in its refurbished space. Now every accoutrement had to have meaning. A crystal vase from a friend brimmed with silks imitating flowers plucked fresh from surrounding fields that no longer existed around my suburban Detroit home, but might have a hundred years before. Blossom-laden, the vase sat atop a garage-sale table that was nicked and scratched but sturdy.

The freshly painted room still lacked soulful purpose until the big chair arrived. Upholstered in more-green-than-blue upholstery to complement the paint job, the pre-washed fabric felt comfortable as old jeans. Overstuffed and plush, the double-wide chair was big enough to curl up and read. A matching ottoman was the same oversized width, and it opened like a trunk to store books and my new collection of antique magazines. It was an oasis of comfort and peace.

*   *   *

Just as I began settling into my new life, the calls began again. The answering machine captured the growing frustration of Mr. Southern Gentleman each time I did not pick up. "C'mon, give me a chance," he said. "You know you're going to give in eventually."

Then one morning at 7:00 a.m., he broke through the message machine's protection. He uncharacteristically called early. Because one of my clients often called before-hours, I thought I better answer. It would be the last call between us.

"Finally," he said. "I thought you disappeared."

In a sense, I had disappeared into painting, decorating and otherwise living. "Disappearing" sounded like I missed something, though, and yet I'd found out so much about myself—about my passion for color and about appreciating the small things like finding a pool of excellent light for reading.

"Do you have everything where you want it now, so we can finally go on a date?" It was hard to believe six months had passed, and now he had no charming left in him. He was blunt, direct. And he acted as if I had been merely organizing a closet.

"I can't. I hate to sound cliché, but it really is me, not you." Maybe I was too dismissive, but I couldn't help myself. "You're a nice guy. You'll find someone."

"But how do you know it's not you, if you've never even tried?" he said. "Look, I don't have my girls this weekend, so it would be perfect. We'll go out and get dinner and see what happens. Let me sweep you off your feet. C'mon."

Now I also had to consider the daughters he might leave behind? I imagined him parking in my driveway in a golden Cadillac, sporting a tail coat and carrying a bouquet under each arm. When we were face-to-face, I knew he would insist we were a pair, and any attempts to shoo him and his many rosebuds out the door would be in vain, like pushing a marshmallow through a straw. No way to push him away once he got close.

"I said *no*. Sorry. Get swept up, get swept under," I barked. He had kids and an ex-wife. He was somebody else's father and husband.

"I don't understand," he said. "All I'm asking is for one night to see how it goes."

"I know you don't understand, and that's the problem," I reasoned with a man to whom I'd spoken only once, and that time the topic had been the many mysteries of X-rated lingerie. I wanted to shout, *Don't call me again. Then there's no disappointment. I need to enjoy my own company and learn who I am. Don't you see? I wasted years—no, decades—ironing shirts for a man who thought me tame and ordinary, not interesting enough to stay around. Could you be the next iron around my neck?* Instead, I let out what I thought was a quick, painless, "I told you no."

"You don't even know me."

"And you don't know me." He was now on the fringe of calling me that name for a snapping female dog, but I didn't care. "Do you realize we haven't even dated yet, and you're already fighting with me. Don't call me anymore." I hung up.

Our notions of how dating would work already conflicted. His idea involved me stuffing myself into a pink-and-black sausage casing and swinging around a pole. Mine included gardens and meadows and cerulean skies. Someone would have to find me there in the light of day, not hidden in the dark of clandestine night.

He also didn't understand my newfound addiction to openness and freedom. If I wanted dinner for lunch . . . wanted to skip dinner altogether . . . or wanted to have a double-chocolate cupcake and diet something to wash it down, I could. I spun my Jewel CD at full-tilt and heard her sing like she knew every note of pain inside me. How did she so completely understand loving someone who didn't love back? I stomped and danced Indian-style around the stereo to Tina Turner classics, affirming that I'm not a fool, merely a woman in love, jilted and re-inventing myself. I would survive Tina style, a bit broken but healing stronger, better than before.

He would never understand my new home as a refuge. One of its three bedrooms housed a new collection of clothing that looked like The New Me, not a woman dressing for a man. A basic black sheath topped with a crisp white blouse tied at the waist and humongous hoop earrings suited me. Maybe some embellished hose. There's something sexy in the initial awakening of senses, like a first kiss, not in the act itself. Dressing had layers like that, too. Underwear was only the beginning, and stripping down was reserved for those who cared enough to take time with outer layers first.

I bagged up and donated any costumes that represented Old Me—the tight-fitting dresses that showed enough cleavage to be tastelessly tasteful. I originally bought the navy blue sequined get-up to match my ex-husband's cummerbund for an awards dinner, a futile attempt to shine alongside him. Now I couldn't stand touching the springy knit that felt like a snake in my hands.

After a month with no calls from Mr. Southern Gentleman, I figured he got the message. Now I could get back into synch with my life. I was an early riser who loved sunrises more than sleep. I watched movies and ate popcorn every Friday in my own private family-room cinema. And for ten years and beyond, I would retreat to my Monet-decorated reading nook. I would curl up in my big chair and read books about abundant spirit and inner light. My life's soundtrack was Eliza Doolittle singing in *My Fair Lady*, "All I want is a room some where . . . with one enormous chair." I was infatuated with the cushy new world I created.

Sitting under *The Japanese Footbridge* enlivened by garden-hued walls, I started down a new emotional path alone, and I never looked back.

Chapter 10

A Couple Dates to Remember (c. 1998)

*T*he first man I dated post-divorce was looking for a dance partner. But he didn't say, "Care to dance?" or "Do you like to dance?" Instead, he asked, "Do you dance?" as if it were a prerequisite.

He wore his private-school tradition and lifestyle from the button-down pink shirt peeking out of his tweed jacket down to his tasseled shoes. Would I call him Phil instead of Peter or Paul, his given biblically inspired name? Worse yet, I might accidentally slip and call him the nickname I had already given him in my head, Prep School.

Fortunately, he did most of the talking. "I need someone to dance with . . . My daughter is getting married in a month . . . I have to do the Father of the Bride dance . . . You know . . . Do you do that kind of dancing?" He said it in one breath, with enough bravado to lead one of his ivy-league cheers.

In asking, at least he finally looked at me for the first time since we got into the car together. Previously, he seemed to be talking to someone just outside the driver-side window.

"Are we going dancing?" I asked. "I thought we were going to the opera."

He said no and "of course not" like it was the most ridiculous question he ever heard.

Prep School obviously missed his deceased wife, but was I already being compared to her? She probably did dance, beautifully, around and *around the country club floor. Maybe that was what he watched in his mind's theater as he stared out the car window—her dancing, her loving their children, or what she looked like the first time they met and she was wearing an adorable, clingy sweater.*

"My wife's been gone two years," he said with a sad, brooding distance. Then he bounced back to cheerfulness again. "You know, the kind (of dancing) they do at Arthur Murray. Ballroom."

I was schooled in rock-n-roll gyrations of the Seventies, so couples dancing meant chipping off twenty years' worth of rust. I also was more likely to break out into Flashdance type movements than I was a waltz. "I don't really dance," I said. Inside I was thinking, I didn't even know you had a daughter. I don't know her name. I keep forgetting your name. Dancing at such an important event? Me?

Apparently, I failed my audition with Prep School. He stared straight ahead as he drove and while at the opera. Without dancing as a topic, there was nothing left to talk about.

The date was a fix-up, and I never heard from Prep School again. So I imagine he found a suitable dance partner. I hope so.

The next time my friend set me up with someone, it was a gay man. He didn't care if I could dance, and he definitely knew how to order from the menu at the pricey Cajun restaurant where the four of us spent too much money on a single meal. We laughed all the way home about our now-depleted credit cards and our narrowly escaping washing dishes. It was a yummy night, with blackened fish, red beans and rice, herb–and dried-tomato-infused cornbread and New Orleans style music (for listening, not dancing).

*   *   *

A few months later, another man I'll call Mr. Perfect pulled his obsessively clean luxury car into my driveway, and so began the fling that was never flung.

He had been my boss fifteen years earlier and was once again in my life, this time as a writing client. When he called to say, "I'm calling about pleasure, not business," I was intrigued and broke my own rule about mixing these polar opposites. He was the strong, silent and successful type that life rewarded because of his manly straightforwardness. I had always liked and respected him, but had never allowed myself to think of him sexually. Now there was that to consider. And we discovered we both divorced about the same time. So why not? Sure.

I don't remember the make or model, but Mr. Perfect's vehicle was a champagne color and drove smooth as a limousine. Night light poured through the moon roof as we drove to downtown Detroit. At the curb of a fabulous jazz restaurant that I wasn't even aware existed (so maybe it was a dream after all?), the doorman called me Mrs. Perfect. This prophecy would evaporate as quickly as the final note on Alexander Zonjic's flute that night, the notes dissipating into the polluted city air.

Mr. Perfect read my mind—savory food with Asian flair and the type of jazz I love, slow and sweet flowing as caramel. We sat elbow-to-elbow on the same side of the table, our arms and legs acting as thermometers to sense any heat we might generate when they accidentally touched. We sipped our sake as if we were in a more exotic world, not merely Motown. Since he lived hours away from the city, I gave him a tour of Detroit architecture. We parked near the waterfront and the towering Renaissance Center, and I pointed out the upper floors, where I worked part-time for an ad agency. We looked across the water at the Canadian shoreline's lights flickering like sunken stars on the Detroit River.

Despite approaching midnight, it was a sunny ride home. He was truly funny; I had never noticed his dry wit before. But crossing the threshold into my house, he grew suddenly and deeply pensive. I kidded that I didn't bite, but suddenly felt like a siren with a sailor, luring him in with the promise of pre-fabricated cappuccino (open packet and pour boiling water). Sorry, there was no French café handy, if that's why he looked unhappier with each sip. Tipping the last drop into his mouth, his smile altogether disappeared, and he rose from the kitchen table to leave. Had a long drive. No kiss. No, no, not too close. It was as if he had promised to be home earlier, and now he was late. It was like someone was waiting up for him.

Within a matter of weeks, I would learn Mr. Perfect was engaged. Was I to have been a last fling, then? The one who finally cemented him to an Unknown Her?

You're welcome, whoever you are.

From Preppy to Perfect, my list of mid-life, post-divorce dating was short but insightful. I still was not ready for the tribulations of dancers, fiancées and flings. I might never be.

Claude Monet. *Cliff Walk at Pourville.* 1882. (Oil on canvas, 66.5 x 82.3 cm.) The Art Institute of Chicago, Chicago, Illinois. Mr. and Mrs. Lewis Larned Coburn Memorial Collection.

Chapter 11

Cliff Walking (c. 2007)

I am drawn to the mystery of the women in Cliff Walk at Pourville. *It hangs near my front door, so every night when I come home, I see the driftwood frame enlivening the aquatic blues and powdery sky into which they gaze without really gazing at all. It's only a framed eight-by-ten version of a much larger original sea-side work in which the Scorpio artist reveals more than his watery, sanguine personality. Monet seems to contemplate something together with the women. Maybe they're thinking of lovers or their place in the vastness of the Atlantic and the universe. It's something not quite within their grasp, but they must figure it out. It's decision time.*

Monet almost depicts how we're all brought to the edge of our innermost selves at times. Painted only a few years after Camille's death, the painting's subjects, who are probably the daughters of the woman who is Monet's lover, stand faceless and motionless like memories to which the artist has not yet committed. Claude Monet and Alice Hoschedé are not yet married. Is he in the process of forgetting Camille? Is he painting the new women into his life? Is this distinction subtle or intense for him?

Like the women on the cliff, I found myself walking the rocky coast of the Greek island of Mykonos in the summer of 2007, pondering a life-changing decision. Tom, my lover for the past year, turned to me and asked, "What do you think about getting married?"

I stopped, unable to move any further down the stone streets. "Now? Here?"

Marriage for the third time, was he kidding? And we had been having such a great time. Now the Greek jewelry stores held more than mere trinkets and souvenirs; my eyes drifted to diamonds and wedding bands. I imagined one fitted to my finger, a telltale sign I would no longer be free to walk alone, even when I wanted.

Falling in love with Tom, I had learned to swim unsure waters all over again. Love can be like landing on a mattress, or it can be free-falling from an airplane. But drowning in it, now that's another matter altogether. When I initially fell for my Scorpio Tom, I sunk like a cork in a whirlpool. I tried staying buoyant, all the while knowing I'd succumb to the spiraling current.

Before Tom and Greece, I had taken "loner trips." I snorkeled off the coast of Cancun, bringing back a conch shell that sat on a table below a small version of Monet's cliff-walking women. My cabbage-sized mollusk constantly reminded me of a day spent mindlessly chasing purple, blue and yellow fish. Sometimes when I looked at *Cliff Walk at Pourville*, I would mentally travel back to the salty air of the harbor outside Boston. I remembered planting my feet to prevent uprooting when a stiff breeze from the over-swelling Atlantic tried to sway me. I would think about whale-watching off the coast of Massachusetts and the gigantic eye of a female breaking the surface and lolling around to catch a glimpse of the tourists on the boat, her baby safe underneath.

Despite my zero-for-two marriage track record, Tom's voice lured me back into the rocky topography of indecision again. Tom played trombone, once with the likes of Ella Fitzgerald, B.B. King, and Aretha Franklin. He taught music for nearly forty years at the college where I now taught English. He sang a little. He conducted an orchestra. He knew harmonies. His voice calmed me.

My Journalism students frequently interviewed Tom for stories they wrote. He was exceedingly affable, encouraging shy students to ask about his orchestra and musical background. When he asked me to attend a concert to thank me for covering of one of his performances, I said yes and was likewise charmed by him. After the show, I found myself with a group of musicians belly-laughing at Tom's endless one-liners. "She was only the farmer's daughter, but she sure could plant two lips." "He's such a bad musician that he can't tune a fish." "How many trumpet players does it take to screw in a light bulb?

Four . . . one to do the work, and three to say how much better they could do it."

Thirteen years my senior, Tom was the type of man who opened doors for me and complimented my jewelry and lipstick shade. He knew his way around dating, so I did wonder how many women there were before me. He wondered about my independence and the fact I only dated twice in ten years.

It would be a third strike for both of us if it doesn't work, I reminded myself and him with every step we took closer to becoming a couple. He also was married twice before.

A few dates later, sexual tension turned up the thermostat twenty degrees during a winter concert. During intermission, to escape the too-close seats, I rushed through the venue's double doors into the frosty night. "Ah, that's better," I said, knowing that as sure as winter would warm up, our physicality would cool down.

"Are you all right?" he asked, holding me.

"I want the first time to be special," I said after the head-rushing, knee-bending kiss that followed.

*   *   *

I still have the dried remains of the two roses Tom placed atop one of the pillows on his bed as a kind of wedding bouquet. Warmed by candlelight and enveloped in eager arms, I was free to unfold like the nearby buds might if they had felt the same warmth.

"Vulnerability" seems inadequate to describe my emotional nakedness and allowing someone to laugh at my birthday suit of foibles and flaws. Safe in a world of my own creation for so long, this six-syllable word does not begin to describe how my life's beautiful balance had toppled. My fear and shaking that first night had less to do with anything my body was experiencing, and more about letting someone make me feel anything emotional. "I feel so vulnerable," I told him, falling like a stone into the sea.

"What can I do to make you feel better?" he asked in that soothing mocha voice.

Tom listened to each new doubt. Telling him expunged some of the dread, allowing it to evaporate into whispers above our now-shared bed. He might get bored with me and put me on a shelf. I'd become Wife in a Jar, pulled out when he needed someone to take out somewhere. Now I was a novelty woman, I told him. While dating, I accessorized head-to-toe in my shiniest, sexiest everything. But how about the reality of me in a well-worn bathrobe? Would he appreciate my blistered hands from working the garden? Would he still tweak my red, runny nose when I had the latest infectious virus? When I was passionate and incensed about issues bothering me, would he love me then as I pounded my fist and screamed the injustice into the stratosphere? Or would he become the fascinated cat playing with a butterfly? With my wings and finery batted off, he might lose interest.

"That's just reality. We'll get through all that," he assured.

Now, for the potential deal-breaker: "Have you ever cheated?" I asked one night during pillow talk. Tongues and truths are freest then.

He could not hide from me. I read his grayish-blue eyes as if they were in a slot machine. If he responded with both irises centered, he told the truth. Eyes darting meant he was lying or retrieving another punch-line as a diversionary tactic.

"How many . . . a hundred?" I half-joked. He also had lived alone ten years.

He wasn't giving numbers, and he wasn't apologizing. "Well, yeah, I might have dated more than one woman at one time. Is that what you mean?" He seemed perplexed by the question, but the eyes remained focused. "Never when I've been married."

Uncomfortable for him. A promise for me.

*   *   *

Now as I stood on tenuous ground in Mykonos a year later, a cloudless sky above and water crashing against the rocks and shore, Tom waited for my reply. I was timelessly suspended like the ladies in *Cliff Walk at Pourville*. Looking out into the blue of sky and sea surrounding the island, I knew whatever I said in that split-second would change the landscape of my life. Jumping into marriage was foolish. But denying myself the beauty found beyond those craggy rocks, azure waves and green grass soaking in sunshine committed an equal sin. Monet made me wonder what lay on the other side of the ocean. Tom had made the possibilities real. I'd always wanted to visit Greece, and here I was.

My first marriage had graduated me from learning geometry in high school to solving problems like doing dishes and pushing a vacuum before I was eighteen. My second marriage started as a hot rush to Sexy Town in a dance club one night, which led to a frozen tundra type of marriage.

As I considered his proposal, my life with Tom so far rushed through my memory. I flashed back to our first trip and the fireworks over the bay in Vancouver, drawing us tight together on the crowded shore as we watched China compete with Sweden to win a prize for musically choreographed, dazzling displays.

The stage was so cavernous the first time we went to The Met in New York, it reminded me of an open-air theatre in the red rocks of America's West.

Tom and I had made new magic under an onyx sky in Montana one night. Transfixed by a big, round moon hanging in the sky and shining a triangular trail of yellow-orange on the lake, I pointed at a flash cutting through the sky's inkiness. "Look at that. I've never seen a shooting star. Have you? Can you see it, right there?"

"I've never seen one either. Are you sure that's what it is?" he asked, knowing nothing else could have created such a perfect tail of light. "Come here," he said, kissing me to mark the moment. It's still my favorite kiss, better than the first because it re-affirmed his intent.

I did not want to taint these memories with negativity. Regardless of these good times we had, that day on Mykonos I began blabbering about prenuptial agreements and the difficulty of selling my house in a bad economy. I could not stop the inertia. The pragmatism of past marriages dragged me down. I doused my Scorpio's flame, nixing an instant Greek wedding.

*　　*　　*

A year later, in the summer of 2008, Tom and I had known each other five years. And though we were not typical marriage candidates, at ages sixty-six and fifty-two respectively, people said we were a "cute couple." We fit. We wished we had met earlier; and we now wanted to enjoy our remaining time together. It seemed an ideal bittersweet premise for a partnership—to live life to the fullest, as long as we could. But something still bothered me. As "I" became "we," would I lose myself again?

On my own, I had started my own writing business. Discovered the rewards of teaching. Earned another degree. Wasted days in the garden. Worked nights to make my home desirable. I developed friendships with people who liked me for who I was, not my identity as the other half of a matched pair. The prenuptial agreement asserted that, yes, what I had achieved would remain mine.

"This all seems so cold," Tom said after re-reading the agreement for the umpteenth time. "You act like you don't trust me. Don't you have any feelings for me at all?"

"Of course I have feelings for you," I argued. "We spend all our free time together. I've practically moved into your house."

"Don't you want to get married ever?" sounded like an ultimatum.

"I'm considering it," I said. And though sadness pulled down the corners of Tom's mouth, I persisted. "Yes, of course I'm thinking about it. We're getting the pre-nups done, aren't we?"

His teary eyes looked into an abyss I could not fathom. "I always wanted the kind of relationship my parents had for sixty years."

He was getting closer to overcoming the final hurdle. "But that's not possible, Dear. Sorry," I said, all the while knowing that past reality had its hooks in me deep.

"I really love you." His eyes wondered if I loved him back.

My heart lurched at the unhappiness I had inflicted . . . his gaze-less gaze and stricken posture slumped in a chair.

"I thought you felt the same about me." He cut to the bone. "I thought we cared for each other. I thought the pre-nups were secondary."

"Don't forget, you have more to lose than I do," I reminded him.

Then a final word tipped the scales. "Don't I make you *happy*? I've never been happier in my life."

"Happy" washed over me like a refreshing shower of rain. Now I realized we had that, and yes, I decided I did want more.

*   *   *

Tom and I stood in a judge's chambers in Ketchikan, Alaska, on August 12, 2008, exchanging vows with words like "forever" and "in sickness and health" and spoke about only the inevitable being able to part us for good. We wanted no fanfare, no real wedding for a couple of odd ducks both married twice before. We threw a bon voyage party with thirty of our closest friends, complete with a boat-decorated sheet cake. A California couple we met in the café on the Alaskan cruise ship witnessed the non-ceremony. And on a typically gray and rainy day for this temperate rain-forest region, we made promises we swore we would keep this time.

There's no evidence that Monet ever saw the glorious glaciers we photographed during our cruise. Alaska was not as popular a destination in the nineteenth century. If the artist had seen them, however, I am sure his palette would have boasted enough shades of blue to paint a frozen heaven.

Our wedding pictures did not reflect a bride and groom who just climbed down from a wedding cake. No flouncy gown or penguin-like tuxedo. A friend told me I should trash the photos taken of the two of us in bus-yellow waders, clumsy rubber boots and rental slickers needed to outfit us for a raft ride down a glacial lake that day. They remain in the photo album anyway. At least our adventure began with genuine smiles and hope.

When we returned from Alaska, a migration of my prized possessions made its way to Tom's place, including clothes, memorabilia and, of course, my Monet prints. As I sketched the layout of placement for my faux art merged with Tom's line drawings of European architecture, a family of our favorite things and places emerged. As I placed each piece in the tiny gallery taking shape in the upstairs hallway of Tom's house, I relived a smidgen of each of the moments represented by my Monet collection. Each print opened a window to my soul over the previous twenty years.

I carefully squared *Cliff Walk at Pourville* on the wall, and I felt my perspective adjust as well. I realized none of us know what lies beyond today's horizon . . . not me, not Tom, not the women on the cliff and not Claude Monet. Not yet sure-footed, I tenuously began looking forward to Tom joining my journey.

Claude Monet. *Sketch of a Figure in the Open Air: Woman with a Parasol Facing Left (Essai de figure en plein-air: Femme à l'ombrelle tournée vers la gauche).* 1886. (Oil on canvas, 131 x 88 cm.) Musée d'Orsay, Paris.

Chapter 12

Paris (c. 2010)

Monet's painting Woman with a Parasol Facing Left *finally comes to life. She turns to look, but not necessarily at me or the artist. Past us. Over our shoulders. Wrapped in a warm breeze, she sees something in the distance or she senses something unseen. I imagine what it's like to be in her laced-up shoes as she visits that place in a woman's heart where she thinks her own thoughts . . . not as a mother, a lover or a wife, but just as herself.*

My first trip to France in 2010 began with an argument between Tom and me. I asserted lingering independence left over from twelve years living alone. Even before the trip, after two years of marriage, we had both begun re-asserting our interests—Tom his music and me writing. Occasionally, our interests conflicted, like our visit to the Louvre, when Tom begged out.

"I know you've seen it before, but I have not," I said, amazed he thought we would visit the periphery of the world's most touted museum without actually going inside.

We had spent our first day in France at Versailles, marveling at its opulence and the acres of gilded and decorated everything. On day two, we meandered through winding streets on Ile St. Louis, sampling food, listening to music, shopping and squeezing each other's hands at each new sensation. That second night we took a slow-moving boat down the Seine to the Eiffel Tower, which sparkled like an architectural constellation made of stars.

Now day three was off to a rocky start. It should have been *the piece de resistance*—the Louvre, Claude Monet and other renowned painters. But *non*? "You're serious. We took the train all the way across the city," I said, "and now all you want to do is look at the buildings?"

"Once you've looked at a few of the main paintings, it's too big to see in a day."

I stood in the Louvre's courtyard looking at the massive series of stone-and-glass structures. I imagined each holding a world of treasures, and I wanted to crack them open like eggs and see the colors inside. "But now we're here and we're not going to see it? Really? You're not kidding?"

"Believe me, you don't want to wait in the lines," he said. "It's the height of tourist season. I'm telling you, it's not worth it. We'll wait forever."

I was a Dorothy wannabe, at the verge of Oz and not able to cross over to the Technicolor spectacle. Tom was my Wicked Witch, keeping me from the rubies and emeralds and everything I'd always known was over the rainbow in France in this very museum. "We'll get a map and only see the good stuff," I said, "you know, like a little painting called the friggin' Mona Lisa."

"You'll never get near it."

"We should have gotten off the train at the secret underground entrance to avoid the lines, like John and Denise told us."

"It will take the whole day out of our schedule. There's so much to see." He opened the guidebook to an earmarked page. "Like Napoleon's Tomb."

Les Invalides was a premier war museum. And the tomb wasn't a tomb at all, but domed statuary full of marble, gilded sculptures and light beams artfully shining on the crypts of famous French dignitaries. I still felt short-changed and forced against my will to spend half a day looking at shiny armor and marble coffins rather than world-renowned paintings. "Napoleon Schnapoleon. Oh yeah, I'd much rather look at armor and swords than beautiful paintings. Then I can tell all my friends how many acres of metal, not art, I saw in France."

I used sarcasm to fight the sting of compromise in this relatively new marriage of mine. Yet it seemed cruel to bring me to the brink of art ecstasy and then retreat. It was sex without the orgasm. I thought about how marriage meant I had to acquiesce now and then. Or did I? Hadn't I already seen more of Paris with Tom than I'd ever imagined? Hadn't we planned another two weeks in the countryside and The Loire Valley?

"Fine, we don't have to go to the Louvre," I mumbled as we slogged back to the train station. "I didn't really want to see the best museum in the world anyway."

Tom had been in charge of planning our Paris trip, using guide books that I only glanced at during the long flight. Grading piles of essays at the end of the semester right before we departed made it prohibitive for me to read anything else. Now, I regretted not taking more time. I should have known he could not be trusted. He knew I wanted to see the Louvre. How could he have missed the hints I had given so overtly so often? And he seemed almost happy about missing it, and, worse, seemed to suggest that waiting in line to realize a long-time dream of mine bordered on ridiculous.

A few stops later, when we disembarked in front of Musée d'Orsay, Tom beamed because his surprise had worked. Turns out, this museum had some of the best Impressionistic art in Paris. Still, some unwritten law of the Universe wanted to keep me from my not-so-secret love, Claude Monet. My enthusiasm (and Tom's) quickly died when we climbed the steps and read "Impressionist exhibit under construction" on a bilingual sign taped to the massive front doors.

Tom turned pale and deeply sighed. "I didn't know. Honestly, I didn't. They're supposed to have lots of Impressionist art. 'The largest collection of Impressionist paintings in the world,'" he read from the guidebook. "Let's go inside."

I fumed. "Fine." I was tired of trains anyway.

No apologies were necessary. The Musée d'Orsay's renovations camouflaged a blessing. The entire Impressionist collection, which I pictured once being scattered about the upper floors like rare trees in a sparsely populated classic-painting forest, had been moved *en masse* to a special exhibit on the lower level, cluttering the space before us with recognizable works of art as far as we could see. Even hallways brimmed with art, recalling the Impressionist movement in its heyday more than a hundred years before. I could practically smell fresh oils and turpentine filling the air with odd perfume, as it might have back then as patrons passed by still-wet paintings.

*　　*　　*

As Tom and I sashay in and out of the galleries, we waltz with dozens of Impressionist paintings. Cézanne's naked ladies dance across the canvasses. Some are cherubic with plump, soft bodies, as if fallen from clouds. In my imagination, jasmine scents Cézanne's heavens, and choirs of seraphim sopranos provide the sound-track.

My loyalty to Monsieur Monet momentarily turns fickle, and I drift toward portraits and sea-scapes by Édouard Manet. What a difference a letter makes. Manet's scenes are darker, more brooding than Monet's. People in his portraits appear sinister and distant, mysterious or maybe on the verge of telling their secrets. I can't be sure. Their questioning eyes and tense body language add a strange liveliness to otherwise foreboding surroundings. I want Manet's subjects to whisper their stories in my ear—not what the painting is "about," but what they are really thinking. Is the sad, subdued woman simply tired, or has she received horrible news that momentarily shocks her? Are the men who are shipping out to sea in a rowboat on a gray rescue mission, or are they defying the tide that has ruined the day's catch?

One step . . . two steps . . . a turn of the corner . . . and a larger-than life Renoir greets me. The young couple dancing together on the enormous canvas looks right at me, as if inviting me to cut in. I imagine an accordion breathing in the laughter of the party-goers and exhaling rich, warm tones of a summer night. I rub my neck at the scratchiness of lace on the woman's dress. Her hand rests on her date's shoulder, his suit probably crumpled from evening dew and perspiration. I visit a time when men hold women like fragile china and use bedroom eyes to seduce them into believing that love begins with a dance. Then a kiss. Maybe more later. Once the music stops, I do not picture the couple relaxing on an armless sofa. Full of energy and fire, and drenched in moonlight, they remain in an active embrace until the final clip-clopping of horse-drawn carriages grows distant and approaching dawn lulls them to sleep.

In another gallery, an especially contemplative work mesmerizes me. Monet's Woman with a Parasol Facing Left *is perched on a hilltop overlooking the summer landscape, maybe the sea. She stands alone in her own thoughts. And I wonder what Monet reveals about relationships as he paints it? I wonder if it's something I can learn, too. I see beyond the mish-mash of pastels in the dress, the umbrella, the hat and the flaxen fields, all blending into this summer dream of a painting. I note Monet's distance and vantage perched below the woman. I appreciate Tom's distance from me now.*

Across the room Tom smiles at me like I am a stranger he casually meets for the first time, but he comes no closer.

Pierre-Auguste Renoir. *Dance in the City (Danse à la ville).* 1883. (Oil on canvas, 181 x 90 cm.) Musée d'Orsay, Paris.

I continue to study the woman that I have only ever seen in miniature before. I begin to understand what Monet already knew. People cannot always be part of a couple. "Together" does not mean constantly conjoined. Separation and even death are as inevitable as sunsets. Monet examines the parasol-toting woman's perspective at the moment. Maybe he wants to see the world through her eyes. But he is not part of her experience. As for the woman, though the artist is nearby, she does not seem to notice, planting her feet on the warm, sure ground. Sun-kissed wind brushes strands of hair across her face. The breeze intoxicates her, and Monet merely plays artistic voyeur during these fleeting seconds of personal bliss . . . rapturous sensations rustling across her skin, awakening her senses. The woman is not purely sexual, but is not asexual either. Ripe as a seed, the lady strolls to this grassy knoll to view the external landscape and, perhaps, reconnects with her own internal rhythms. The season smacks of blossoms and wine. Birds squawk overhead. Someone crunches an apple fresh from a tree. Girlish laughter carries on the wind. She sighs deeply.

I looked at Tom. Not a big Impressionist fan (he prefers Baroque art and music), he pretended to be engaged in viewing one of Monet's renditions of Rouen Cathedral, one of the many stops on our itinerary. He nodded, but stayed where he was, allowing me to enjoy my art find alone. He waited for a signal that my Monet fix had contented me.

I walked nearby and whispered, "This is perfect, as if they've put out the best of the best just for us."

"So, now you're glad we missed the Louvre?"

"What could top this?" I sidled up next to him, grabbed his hand, and rested my head on his shoulder.

I should have known things would work out where Monet was concerned. It usually does. At first, when we bypassed the Louvre, I thought that Tom simply wanted to control me like other men in my past. A surprise like Musée d'Orsay knocked me off kilter. Old habits like mistrust and confusion had resurfaced, but now they had melted away, and the whole trip—the whole world—looked brighter.

I glanced at the lady with a parasol one more time. She was strong and sure in her stance.

*   *   *

As Tom and I left the museum that day, the conversation turned to food.

"Do you think we could we find some of those giant crepes again? Or how about that vegetarian place with the chewy bread?" I was reinvigorated about anything French.

"Or, maybe we can just wander Champs-Élysées and see what we find. It doesn't really matter, does it?"

He was right. "Sure, let's walk. Maybe we can buy some more *souvenirs*," I said, knowing how much he hated shopping.

"Maybe," he said, with a weightiness given to this non-committal word that suggested there were more surprises to come. We would have to wait and see.

We sashayed down winding sidewalks past statue–and filigree-embellished bridges. We followed the friendly river, and again found ourselves among hoards of people, all searching for something but not knowing exactly what. The café menus would tempt us to indecision until we found a delicacy we couldn't resist.

"This one has a salad with baked brie on top. I love the cheese here," I said of my latest food fetish.

"Look, this one has a seafood dish with everything but the kitchen sink in it. Maybe some seafood?" he suggested.

We finally settled into comfy chairs outside a café that provided the ideal spot to watch a sunset and eat pasta served with crusty bread. As the Paris sky filled with neon blue and pink, highlighting a slip of an emerging moon, sparrows pecked crumbs at our feet. Tom sipped his wine, and I swigged foam from my latte. Plates rattled inside the restaurant. People chattered on the street and all around, ambient mutterings of love and life passing between them. Tom massaged my neck, loosening its tight chords and relaxing my shoulders. I put my hand on his warm thigh in anticipation of curling up next to him that night. We indulged in a kiss deep enough that I picked up my menu and hid our faces.

"We are too old. People will see," I said.

"Who cares?"

We kissed deeper and stronger, exchanging "I love you."

Some moments I would like to bottle and save, or have them painted onto a canvas so I can relive them again and again.

Epilogue

Any attempt to vilify, saint, or otherwise dehumanize any character in this book was not intentional. While the events are real, some of the names have been changed to protect those who are not as ready to tell the story as I.

Readers of my early drafts found the writing very honest, and that has been the guiding force of this book.

My father used to say, "There's a little larceny in all of us," and I live by that motto. In my mind, what choice do I have? Human beings are so imperfect, it makes perfect sense that flaws contribute to the overall character of each person. As a writer and a humanist, I wouldn't have it any other way. I have written about aspects of my marriages and people I've known throughout my life, and I have often revealed my own imperfections in the process.

I do not pretend that my journey is finished or that my current marriage is tied up with a nice, neat ribbon. I don't truthfully know what the future holds for Tom or me. The only thing that I do know is that like my hero Claude Monet, only the constant pursuit of beauty, love, and light can help bring these things into the world.

I continue to be awed by Monet's artful perseverance.

* * *

References

Books and Web

Claude MONET Paintings by Claude Oscar Monet. Web. 04 Jan. 2012.
<http://www.intermonet.com>.

Giverny Vernon: In the Heart of Impressionism. Web. 04 Jan. 2012.
<http://www.giverny.org>.

Heinrich, Christoph. *Claude Monet, 1840-1926.* San Diego, CA:
Thunder Bay, 1997. Print.

Joyes, Claire, and Claude Monet. *Claude Monet: Life at Giverny.* New
York: Vendome, 1985. Print.

Madeline, Laurence, and Margaret Rocques. *100 Impressionist
Masterpieces: Musée D'Orsay.* Paris: Éd. Scala, 2010. Print.

Robinson, William H. *Monet to Dalí: Impressionist and Modern
Masterworks from the Cleveland Museum of Art.* Cleveland, OH:
Museum, in Association with Hudson Mills, 2007. Print.

Spate, Virginia. *Claude Monet: Life and Work, with over 300 Illustrations,
135 in Colour.* New York: Rizzoli, 1992. Print.

Stuckey, Charles F., Claude Monet, and Sophia Shaw. *Claude Monet:
1840-1926.* New York: Thames and Hudson, 1995. Print.

Paintings

Monet, Claude. "A Corner of the Apartment." 1875. Painting. *Musée
d'Orsay.* Web. 15 January. 2012.

Monet, Claude. "Camille Sur Son Lit De Mort (Camille Monet on her
Deathbed)." 1879. Painting. *Musée d'Orsay.* Web. 15 January. 2012.

Monet, Claude. "Cliff Walk at Pourville." 1882. Painting. *The Art Institute of Chicago.* Web. 15 January. 2012.

Monet, Claude. "Essai de figure en plein-air: Femme à l'ombrelle tournée vers la gauche (Sketch of a Figure in the Open Air: Woman with a Parasol Facing Left)." 1886. *Musée d'Orsay.* Web. 25 January. 2012.

Monet, Claude. "Garden at Sainte-Adresse." 1867. Painting. *The Metropolitan Museum of Art (metmuseum.org).* Web. 15 January. 2012.

Monet, Claude. "La Corniche Near Monaco." 1884. Painting. *Rijksmuseum (rijksmuseum.nl).* Web. 15 January. 2012.

Monet, Claude. "Nympheas (Waterlilies)." 1914-1915. Painting. *Portland Art Museum.* Web. 15 January. 2012.

Monet, Claude. "Poppies at Argenteuil." 1873. Painting. *Musée d'Orsay.* Web. 15 January. 2012.

Monet, Claude. "Sunset on the Seine in Winter." 1880. Painting. Private Collection *(monetpainting.net).* Web. 15 January. 2012.

Monet, Claude. "The Artist's Garden at Vétheuil." 1880. Painting. *National Gallery of Art, Washington.* Web. 15 January. 2012.

Monet, Claude. "The Ice Floes (Les Glacons)." 1880. Painting. *Shelburne Museum.* Web. 15 January. 2012.

Monet, Claude. "The Japanese Footbridge and the Water Lily Pool, Giverny." 1899. Painting. *Philadelphia Museum of Art.* Web. 15 January. 2012.

Monet, Claude. "The Parc Monceau." 1876. Painting. *The Metropolitan Museum of Art (metmuseum.org).* Web. 15 January. 2012.

Monet, Claude. (French, 1840-1926). *The Red Kerchief,* ca. 1868-1873. Oil on fabric, 99.0 x 79.8 cm. The Cleveland Museum of Art. Bequest of Leonard C. Hanna, Jr. 1958.39.

Renoir, Pierre-Auguste. "Danse à la ville (Dance in the City)." 1883. Painting. *Musée d'Orsay.* Web. 25 January. 2012.